KU-714-601

THE TURN OF THE TIDE

THE TURN OF THE TIDE
Christian Belief in Britain Today

KEITH WARD

BBC PUBLICATIONS

Published by BBC Publications
A division of BBC Enterprises Ltd
35 Marylebone High Street, London W1M 4AA

ISBN 0 563 20501 6

First published 1986
© Keith Ward 1986

Typeset in 9/11 Palatino by Wilmaset, Birkenhead, Wirral
Printed in Great Britain by Cox & Wyman

CONTENTS

PREFACE

This is a very much expanded version of a series which first appeared on BBC Radio Four in the spring of 1986. The general aim is to present a view of the state of Christian belief in Britain. It is not meant to give a sort of survey of what British people believe, in general; nor is it primarily concerned with such things as church attendance or psychological reasons for being Christian. I have touched on those things very briefly. But my main concern is with the *beliefs* of Christians, in what is often said to be a secular and post-Christian culture. How do these beliefs shape up against the best modern scientific knowledge? Against the criticisms of philosophers? Has Christian morality collapsed? Have traditional beliefs been undermined by Biblical criticism and by the rejection of orthodox doctrines like the Trinity and the incarnation? Has Christianity in Britain just become one among many religions, all open to personal choice? And have Christians had to give up their beliefs about supernatural realities, and replace them with rather amateurish political commitments?

Those are the questions with which I have been mainly concerned. What I have tried to do is go to the leading authorities in various fields, people who are Christians but are undisputed leaders in their own fields of scholarship, whether it is physics or philosophy or theology. In a series of interviews with them, I have tried to build up a picture of how Christians see their own beliefs in the light of the best knowledge in their own special fields.

I have included one or two of the best-known non-Christians, primarily to show how Christians in the same field respond to them. I am not pretending that Christian belief can now be seen by all intelligent people to be overwhelmingly probable. That would be wholly false. But I have discovered that Christians are not so much on the defensive as may be thought. There is a weaker and a stronger conclusion that I propose. The weaker one is that Christian belief, or at least some forms of it, is quite compatible with scientific and philosophical knowledge and acceptance of all the critical techniques of modern scholarship. I have found it fascinating to see how Christian physicists, biologists and philosophers give an account of their faith, and show how their own research has contributed to it.

The stronger conclusion is that the progress of knowledge in the sciences, in philosophy and in theology itself has actually made Christian belief seem much more acceptable now than it might have seemed forty or fifty years ago. It is in this respect that I suggest that the tide has turned from a rejection of religious belief to a greater openness towards it. Christian belief is actually in quite a strong position as far as the intellectual arguments go. But of course they do not go very far; and perhaps most people are not fully aware of them. So it is not a question of everybody flooding back to the churches. Intellectual fashions come and go; and the new intellectual strength of Christian belief may be just another swing of the pendulum of fashion. But I do not think so; it seems to me that certain basic positions have now been established. Just as we can never go back before the Enlightenment; so we cannot now return to the easy scepticism of the early twentieth century. That is what has been decisively overthrown.

I do not believe that Christianity stands or falls by its intellectual strength. But it does seem to me that if it is demonstrably weak, intellectually, that should weaken a reasonable person's adherence to it. And if it is true, then it ought to be intellectually strong; that is, there should be some good arguments for it. So perhaps it is not entirely unimportant to show that it has intellectual strength. And that is what I have called my expert witnesses to show.

I would like to record my thanks to all those who allowed themselves to be interviewed. I believe I have not misinterpreted them; but they are not responsible for any of the general conclusions I draw from my talks with them. I would like to thank David Winter, Head of Religious Broadcasting, and David Craig, of the BBC, for first encouraging my work on the series. David Peet and Iuen Russell-Jones, of BBC Wales, produced it. As a member of the Church in Wales in exile, I deeply appreciated their work. Susan Kennedy, of BBC Publications, was enormously helpful in turning the series into this book, as was my wife Marian, who endured several unreadable versions. And Julie McRae typed it out with fewer mistakes than I put into it. I am very grateful for all their help.

Chapter One
THE TURN OF THE TIDE

Is there a future for Christianity in Britain? To many people it seems that Britain is an almost wholly secular and post-Christian country. Christian belief seems, like many other values and beliefs of the Victorian age of Empire, a faded and tattered relic of a half-regretted, half-respected past. It still provides pretty weddings, dignified funerals and grand state occasions. But otherwise it is very much a minority interest for those, mostly women, who like that sort of thing. There is virtually no serious discussion of it at any intellectual level higher than that of the primary school. Even though, by the 1944 Education Act, religion is a compulsory subject in schools, it is not taught at all in most secondary schools beyond the third grade. And very often, when it is taught, it consists largely of ill-informed discussions on what various members of the class think of peace, abortion or women's rights.

By the time pupils get to the fifth and sixth forms, they are often informed that religion is not an intellectual subject, so it should not be taken for O or A levels, unless they really cannot think of anything decent. Discussion in the media, with some honourable exceptions, is often confined to gossip about the more provocative statements of clerics; or to discussions by sophisticated atheists who manage to give the impression that religion is some sort of superstitious relic which needs explaining, but is not worthy of understanding. I recently heard an allegedly serious television discussion on religion which was conducted by three atheists and a theologian so radical that he kept telling the atheists they believed too many things. So it is easy to get the impression that Christian faith is a thing of the past; fairy-tales and legends to help sales at Christmas, but not a matter for serious intellectual discussion.

Now in this book I aim to show that this impression is completely false. There are strange stirrings of life even in that arthritic old body of the Church of England. Things have changed almost out of recognition in the last few years, in science, in philosophy, in theology and in moral thinking.

9

There has been a revolution in thought, not yet widely recognised, which has unsettled our recently acquired certainties about the ultimate and exhaustive truth of science, and which has brought religious belief back to the forefront of the intellectual scene. Most people, when they talk about new thought, are talking about the thought that was new when they were young – that is, thirty years or so ago. The high-point of atheism in Britain was about fifty years ago, in fact. I would date it to coincide with the publication of a little bombshell of a book, *Language, Truth and Logic* by the philosopher A. J. Ayer. And that is where many people have stayed. But things have moved on a very long way since then. Ayer, about whom I shall be talking in more detail in chapter three, has long since renounced much of what he then said. He has not by any means ceased to be an atheist. But it has perhaps become clearer that his atheism was not really founded on the arguments of that book; nor I should think on any particular intellectual arguments at all.

I am not going to hold that atheism has been refuted; that would be silly; it is not refutable, any more than theism is. But I do think that the arguments which have been used to undermine belief in God can now be seen not to have the overwhelming force they were at one time thought to have. And there are clear signs in the intellectual life of our culture of a return to religious beliefs and values. Or perhaps I should say, not so much a *return* as a rethinking and reshaping which uses all the insights of the scientific and critical revolutions and seeks to move on to a fuller and more comprehensive vision of human life which will include the spiritual dimension as well as the material.

I am a Christian, and I do not claim to be some kind of totally impartial intellect, surveying the British scene with omniscient wisdom. But I do not believe anyone is truly impartial in such matters; and one may as well be honest about where one starts. Nevertheless, I have not always been a Christian. Like most people of my generation in Britain, I passed through a phase of happy atheism. I did not become a Christian because of any need or emotional turmoil – unless it was, perhaps, that I became dissatisfied with my own self-satisfaction. I became a Christian very largely because I came to believe that the intellectual leading-edge of debate in fact lay with Christianity; that its claim to truth was an eminently plausible one; and that it was much the most fascinating, difficult and yet rationally stimulating vision of the world.

In this book I am going to try to be fair in presenting a view of the role and intellectual vigour of the Christian churches in Britain today. I will seek to marshal arguments from the sciences, philosophy, ethics, politics, historical and literary criticism, and from theology itself, which show the state of play in Christian thought in Britain in the late twentieth century. I think there may be a few surprises for those who think that Christianity is washed up or played out. There may even be a few surprises for Christian believers, who have not been aware of what has been going on, of the new and exciting developments that have been taking place over the last few years. Because I think there can be no doubt that the Christian faith has passed through one of those great revolutions that have periodically transformed it, throughout the two thousand years of its existence. Revolutions take a bit of adjusting to; and this one will take decades to sink in. But it has happened; and what it has left is a new reinvigorated form of faith. It is strong enough to challenge the presuppositions of anyone who looks carefully at it. It is fascinating and exciting enough to arouse the enthusiasm of anyone who cares about truth and understanding. It looks like something new and creative, with a positive future before it.

That, at any rate, is the view I will be putting forward. But I must begin with a candid and indeed inescapable confession. If we are looking at the state of Christianity in Britain today, we must look at the actual state of the churches. And if we just look there, and do not probe far beneath the surface, things can look pretty depressing. All those huge, half-empty churches, with signs outside asking for money to keep them from falling down, give more an impression of a religion in decay, than of anything vital and alive. Institutional Christianity is, indeed, in trouble. According to one summary of church statistics for 1980, only 17 per cent of the United Kingdom are members of Christian churches. That is just under a fifth of the population, which does make Christians very thin on the ground.

To some extent, of course, the Protestant churches, at least, are themselves responsible for this. It has been a feature of Protestantism to stress that each individual can be directly related to God; that there is no need of any institution or hierarchy to mediate between man and God. Salvation is by faith alone; so you can believe in your heart, and do not need to attend church to be present at Mass or go to Confession, for example. It is not surprising that many people have heard this message, and decided that they need not bother to attend or join a church at all. So, if you look at the number of people who claim to be Christians, you get a much higher figure than the number of church-goers. About 60 per cent of the population of Britain are baptised as Christians. And about 77 per cent of the population say they believe in God (Gallup Poll, 1968; confirmed by University of Leeds Research, 1982) – though it might be best not to enquire too closely what they mean by 'God'. In the Leeds survey, 43 per cent of the sample said that they believed Jesus was the Son of God; and 24 per cent – almost a quarter – said that religious belief was 'very important' to them.

It may be true that basic religious beliefs in God and in such things as life after death have declined a little in this century; but not, it seems, to any significant extent. Atheism is something which is espoused by only about 10 per cent of the population; David Martin, Professor of Sociology at the London School of Economics, engagingly describes it as 'froth amongst the intelligentsia'. The big decline has been in relation to the specific institutions of Christianity, the churches, a process that Professor Martin sums up: 'It's reasonable to say that up to the First World War, the Christian churches were holding up fairly well. That war meant a shattering of their confidence and it ate very seriously into their organisation. Then there was a stabilisation in the twenties; and after that a decline in the thirties. There was a general mood of cultural crisis in which the churches were involved. After the Second World War there was yet another period of relative stability, a sort of plateau. Then, in the 1960s, there was a further cultural crisis; and the decline in the churches has continued, with a slight bottoming out at the end of the seventies. Maybe the decline has now resumed.' For example, such things as baptisms, weddings and funerals – what sociologists call 'rites of passage' – have declined since the sixties by anything from a third to a half.

This long decline during this century has not been confined to the churches. There has, Professor Martin pointed out, been a general erosion of participation in all kinds of activities, especially since the sixties, whether one is talking about football, or films, or political meetings, or attendance at trade

THE TURN OF THE TIDE

union meetings. But maybe there is more to it than that. 'There is another area of cultural crisis; and that is in terms of morals, manners, expectations, attitudes towards the law; all those things have changed since the sixties. So it's not simply the decline in attendance at particular kinds of meeting. It's a loss of general social confidence.'

To back up this assertion, Professor Martin draws attention to such things as the European Values Survey, which has been conducted over the last five years in several countries, including Great Britain. 'What it shows is that, although politically there has been a return in recent years to govern-ments of conservative character, which have emphasised law and order, culturally the shifts of the sixties have tended to continue. When people approach questions relating to the moral order, they have largely hedonistic attitudes based on their own calculations of personal happiness, rather than on some notion of obeying an objective law. So in that area of moral practice, there has been a continuing crisis; and the decline of the churches has been a further aspect of that.'

Of course, you may well feel it is a matter of opinion that this stress on personal happiness is any sort of crisis. You may think it is a healthy individualism. But it must be admitted that, if most people are seeking their own individual happiness first, it will be much harder to get any sense of social cohesion or a shared vision of a just society. I have noticed myself, when giving talks to various groups around the country, that if I am making a list of moral values, I often have to cross words like 'patriotism' and 'duty' out. To many people, such things just don't seem to be values any more, whereas at one time they were taken to be basic foundations of British life. Something has definitely changed; maybe we can reserve judgement on whether it's good or bad, for the moment. But it obviously makes belief in a God who might have some sort of objective law in mind, or the practice of church-going, which does not seem to offer suitably large doses of pleasure, much less popular.

On the other hand, if we take a rather longer view, maybe the position today is not entirely new. Professor Martin suggests, 'If one goes back to the eighteenth century, or the beginning of the nineteenth, one discovers very low levels of rather passive practice. I think that if you had gone back to Oxfordshire in the late eighteenth century, you would find that levels of attendance were not so very different than they are now. And if you go back further in British history – let's say, to the late Middle Ages – you would have to ask questions about how much people even knew about the fundamentals of Christianity, and how much it was all mixed up with the general processes of social conformity and government.' This suggests that the decline in practice is not a quite new and unprecedented move away from religious belief, a sort of escape from superstition into a golden age of reason. It is more like a return to lethargy, after a rather unusual bout of piety in the late nineteenth century.

The Christian churches cannot be considered in isolation from the culture of which they have been such an important part. Just as our traditional culture has changed very rapidly in this century, has lost its imperial status and is still seeking a new role, so, perhaps, the Christianity which was so bound up with that culture is suffering from a similar loss of status and lack of a clear self-image or conception of its role in national and international affairs. We are now presiding over the funeral rites of imperial Christianity. And this decline is not just a British phenomenon; it is part of a more general European decline. What is interesting is that this decline is contrasted with American buoyancy. When sociologists are speculating, as from time to time they do, they wonder if the overall buoyancy of America, that is to say, its dominant world-position and a sense of a future in front of it, has not got something to do with the buoyancy of its religion. The general sense of unease and uncertainty and of post-imperial dejection in Europe correlates strongly with a sort of religious dejection and pessimism. There is a very big contrast between the American and the British and European situation.

The four countries which comprise the United Kingdom are of course significantly different from each other in their attitudes to Christian institutions. The highest rate of participation in Christian rites is in Northern Ireland; but in that country, a state of virtually open warfare exists between Roman Catholics and Protestants. The linking of political and religious attitudes is particularly clear there; and, whatever the leaders of the Christian denominations say, religious affiliation is widely used as a means of determining membership of irreconcilable political groups, locked in a circle of mutual hatred and destructiveness. Most people in England, Scotland and Wales regard the situation with bewildered horror; it certainly contributes to a general sense of despair and cynicism about Christianity. Where people preach a religion of love, and murder each other on the streets, it hardly looks as if the Christian faith has anything positive to offer in social or moral affairs. In Northern Ireland, the Christian faith has virtually destroyed its own credibility in a torrent of religiously sanctioned bigotry and violence.

In Wales, the situation is quite different. The Church in Wales was disestablished in 1920, so there is no established church. That Church has to a large extent been associated in the minds of many Welsh people with a disliked English ascendancy, and the soul of Wales was found largely in the thousands of Protestant Chapels of many different denominations. With their great emphasis on Bible reading and preaching, the Chapels educated masses of young working people and then exported them to other countries, leaving the Chapels empty and forlorn. Today, Wales is a country very much still in search of its proper character, torn between nationalism and internationalism, love for Welsh culture and desire to participate more fully in a wider community. The Welsh churches, having played a major role in forming Welsh culture in the past, are now caught up in the same tensions and confusions as the country as a whole, and are unable to distinguish clearly between insular obscurantism and a positive development of the creative resources of Welsh culture. Sadly, perhaps the major symbols of Welsh Christianity today are the vast empty Chapels which litter the mining valleys, as deserted as the mineshafts which lie beneath them.

Scotland is different again. Since the Reformation, it has been strongly Presbyterian in character, and the Church of Scotland is established by Scottish law as the religion of the country, with the monarch pledged to preserve its form of government and system of beliefs. The level of participation in Christian activities is markedly higher in Scotland than in England (37 per cent church membership, as compared with 13 per cent). In general, however, the Scottish situation is most similar to that in England, where the Church of England is established by law, and the monarch is its supreme governor in matters temporal and ecclesiastical. The monarch thus has the great distinction of being a Presbyterian in Scotland and an Episcopalian in England. It is worth pointing out, however, that, even though the forms of church government differ, both these national churches would claim to be quite properly part of the one true Catholic Church of Christendom, and a genuine successor to the first apostolic community.

Even though England is the most highly secularised part of the United Kingdom, it remains very much a Christian country in law. Twenty-six bishops sit by right in the House of Lords, and Parliament has its Chaplain and opens with prayers every day. The teaching of religion is compulsory in schools; and there is still a law of blasphemy, which specifically forbids attacks on the doctrines of the Church of England. Perhaps it is part of our post-imperial puzzlement that the English do not quite know what to do with the establishment. They are not sure whether they want it or not; or even exactly what it is and what difference it makes. It is worth looking in a little more detail at the situation in England, as an illustration of the very complex relation between culture and belief.

Some people think that the Church of England was founded by Henry VIII because he wanted a divorce and the Pope would not give him one. The easiest way out of his problem was to start his own church; so he did. That is a travesty of the truth, of course; and, as usual in English history, the whole thing is so complicated as to be almost impenetrable. But it is clear that the Church of England claims that its bishops, or chief ministers, are properly and duly commissioned by the successors of the original twelve apostles. What it does not admit – and here it agrees with the many Eastern Orthodox churches – is that the Bishop of Rome, the Pope, has the sort of supreme authority or infallibility given to him by the Roman communion. As the Prayer Book puts it, 'The Bishop of Rome hath no jurisdiction in this realm.' The break with Rome was an argument about authority and sovereignty. It was not just about divorce; it was a messy and complicated matter involving the payment of church taxes, the appointment of bishops and the relationship of church and state. When the monarch of England took the title of supreme governor of the church, he was not claiming to be the head of the church, in the sense of its spiritual leader. He was trying to settle once and for all the old argument about who had supreme authority in the state. Like many other rulers in many other countries – in fact, like the Emperor Constantine in the fifth century – Henry claimed jurisdiction over all matters temporal and ecclesiastical. That is, he could control church property, the appointment of bishops and regulate forms of service. But he could not alter doctrines; and he certainly did not intend to found a new church. He wanted to exercise temporal authority over the Church in England, and reject the Pope's claims in that respect.

On any coin of the realm you will find the letters 'FD' after the name of the sovereign. That means *'Fidei Defensor'* Defender of the Faith; and it was, ironically, the title given to Henry VIII by Pope Leo X for writing a book in defence of the seven sacraments. It is still kept by English monarchs to symbolise their position as defenders of the Christian Faith. After the initial break with Rome, the English Church was transformed by the Prostestant Reformation; and now the monarchs of Great Britain and Northern Ireland are bound to defend the Protestant faith, as it is understood in the Church of England and the Church of Scotland. But their position is not comparable in any way to that of the Pope. It is temporal authority over and responsibility for the institution of the established churches in Britain. But they have no authority at all for promulgating authoritative teaching on faith or morals, or for being supreme pastors or priests in the church.

John Gladwin, who is secretary of one of the most important Boards of the Church of England, the Board of Social Responsibility, views the role of the monarch thus: 'The Queen in Parliament is responsible for the government of the church. The Queen focuses formally what the constitution of our nation is, and the church is part of this. That does not mean that she personally governs the Church of England or issues direct orders as to what we should or shouldn't do. But there are agreed ways in which the church is to be governed. Changes have to be agreed through Parliamentary legislation, which, in the end, she has to put her signature to, if they are to become law.' In practice, this means that the Prime Minister of the day exercises some influence, especially in the appointment of bishops. John Gladwin has his own summary of this procedure: 'The church has a way of forming its mind on the matter; and then the state responds, as the constitution requires.' What actually happens is that there is a senior civil servant who receives names of possible bishops, and presents them to the Prime Minister in a preferred order. There is an informal understanding that she will accept them in that order; but she could in principle refuse to do so, and place a veto on one or other name. There are also laws governing matters like church worship, forms of worship and so on. And changes in those laws require parliamentary consent. One result of this could be the situation – on the face of it, rather odd – where Members of Parliament with little or no religious interest at all were making decisions which affected a church of which they were not members.

John Gladwin does not apparently see this as a serious problem, although he accepts that it could happen. 'If the government decided to take the church head on, as it were, then we would have a constitutional crisis, which would involve both the church and the monarchy . . . At the moment there is no sign of such a crisis developing. Everybody abides by carrying out their particular part in the process.' What that has meant in recent years is that the church wanted to propose new forms of worship; Parliament rejected the idea; and the church went ahead, calling them not 'new' but 'alternative'. A typical British compromise, indeed!

The possibilities of collapse are enormous. What if Prince Charles, or a successor of his, decided to join the British Humanist Association, or even become a Buddhist? What if Parliament voted to abolish public acts of worship altogether? What if the Prime Minister refused to appoint any of the church's nominees as a bishop? The answer seems to be, as in so many other things, that to the British, the improbable is unthinkable, so we need not bother about it. Like so many of our institutions, if we could start again from scratch, we would probably not choose this one. But, like Topsy, it has just growed; it's most unlikely to be totally dismantled; so we may as well make the best of it. 'Its importance is that it is part of the culture we live with; the church has a particular image on formal occasions and a part formally in the life of the nation. So our culture and our history has been greatly affected by that. It is an important part of British life. What one's judgement on it might be is a matter for debate; but of its importance I think we ought not to be in doubt.'

The apologetic tone of John Gladwin's comment is interesting; as if the speaker sensed that the cultural image presented by the church might be regarded with some scepticism by many. I am reminded of a Remembrance Day service I once attended, at which there was a curate who had very long hair; and one of the splendid veterans in the congregation said, rather volubly, 'That's not a parson; it's a hippy.' It seems that one of the great problems confronting the Church of England, at least, is uncertainty about what exactly it is. Does it exist to perform the encrusted rituals of our imperial past? Or is it a group of rather radical and critical bishops, apt to cause the government aggravation and annoyance? The trouble is that it is both. In other words, the Church reflects the confusion of the country as a whole about its role and image in the world.

In fact, the Church of England has always failed in its self-allotted task of being the church of all the English people. The nonconformist churches – Baptists, Methodists, United Reformed and many others – have played a most significant part in making the British character what it is. They have preserved traditions of greater radicalism and independence from matters of state, and have been less associated with the hierarchy of British society. And the Roman Catholic Church, after the Emancipation Act of 1829, expanded very rapidly until the 1960s when it joined the other churches in the present decline. There are many varieties of Christianity in Britain, and that, too, exacerbates the problem of giving the faith a clear role and image. Some of the smaller groups, like the Unitarians, are on the verge of extinction, while others exist in fairly small numbers. If we look at some recent figures, about 1,200,000 people are usually present at Sunday services in the Church of England. The Roman Catholic Church in Britain as a whole has an average Sunday attendance of 1,500,000. The Church of Scotland has 1 million; Baptists and the United Reformed Church attendances average about 150,000 each. Out of a population of 55 million, these numbers are rather small. They lead one to look at some of the other religions which now exist in Britain. For though Christianity is still the largest religion, it is not by any means the only one. There are said to be about 1½ million Muslims; and according to a survey carried out in 1985, they have just under 300 registered mosques. That turns out to be about the same as the number of church-going Anglicans, though admittedly it is rather unfair to compare regular church-goers with people who may be only Muslim by birth, but do not practise their religion. There are also about 400,000 Jews and the same number of Sikhs; and so both those groups outnumber the combined forces of Baptists and United Reformed Church members. It seems that, from the point of view of religious allegiance, modern Britain is indeed a plural society, with the majority of people showing a vast indifference to organised religion. It is not that atheism is strong. The diverse and generally tolerant nature of Christianity in Britain does not breed strong antagonism. In fact, in some ways, religion could be said to be flourishing. Peter Clarke, of the Centre for the Study of New Religious Movements at King's College, London, has on file over 450 new religions. These religions may claim to be as old as the Pyramids – in fact, many of them claim to be even older – but they have arrived in Britain since 1945.

Peter Clarke hears of new ones every day: 'In the sixties they were quite successful in attracting people, and up to the middle seventies. But I do not think the majority of them are successful, and most are now in a sort of decline.' That sounds a familiar story. 'What we see in the older ones, like Hare Krishna or the Unification Church, is a steady growth, slow but steady. The most successful of all are the Indian new religions, of which we have many – the Satya Sai Baba movement, Brahma Kumaris and a variety of others.' This is certainly an explosion in terms of religions, if not of numbers of adherents, and it stands in need of some explanation. Peter Clarke suggests that religious knowledge is regarded as some form of deviant knowledge: 'It is hidden or kept under the carpet, because everything is supposed to be governed by rational thought and science. I think there is a high degree of religious awareness around which is muffled or suppressed. What is happening is that this is being exploited by these new religions. There is a market, and these religions are going into it, and drawing out of people what they have always felt they ought to keep quiet about. Maybe the churches are not catering for this religious awareness. In the Christian tradition there is a strong emphasis on the value of religious awareness and experience, on mysticism. But it is probably not being put across to the same extent as, say, the social gospel.'

Here is another factor to add to our account of religious decline. Not only is there a crisis of confidence culturally, and an insecurity about the role and image of the churches in society, but people are actually embarrassed to admit that they have religious feelings. Yet there is considerable evidence to suggest that they do. Sir Alister Hardy, founder of the Religious Experience Research Unit at Oxford, has carried out an extensive programme of research on people's beliefs and attitudes. He finds that a very large number of people do experience what he describes as a sense of a higher benevolent power, in a number of ways. But they rarely associate this experience with the beliefs expressed by any church; and in fact it quite often seems to put them off going to a church ever again.

There seems to have developed a sort of split between religious experiences and the systems of dogma which the churches are thought to be propounding. In the words of Peter Clarke: 'There seems to have been a collapse of religious belief in the sense that there no longer exists, to the same extent as in the past, a coherent system of beliefs. Christians will mix belief in reincarnation with belief in Jesus as Saviour. There are Christian gnostics, who believe that all evil is due to ignorance; and yet hold at the same time that they are saved by the death and resurrection of Jesus. There is often a mélange of beliefs in people's minds. So there is no longer a schematic, coherent system of dogmas; but I would have thought that people are having religious feelings to the same extent as before.'

People still have the same sort of religious feelings, then; but they feel uncomfortable with what they see as the irrational or anti-scientific dogmas of the churches. On the other hand, the new religions do not provide anything more rational; and when they use scientific-sounding jargon, it is almost always pseudo-science, a mixture of balderdash and gobbledegook. Peter Clarke again: 'I don't think new movements are giving people something that they can grasp intellectually. They are not about reason, about whether something is actually true or false. They are much more about techniques and methods to acquire spiritual awareness, to improve oneself and so on. Many of them offer very little at the intellectual level; and this is not necessarily in conflict with what people want in a scientific age. Many people have decided that the rational approach to truth is a dead-end anyway. Religion is incompatible with the scientific world-view; so if we are going to have religion, we may as well have it for emotional reasons.'

Here, in a way, is the heart of the matter. Religious beliefs just do not seem to fit into the scientific world-view. So they are either repressed, or they are adopted for purely emotional reasons. At the same time, religion is becoming increasingly privatised, an area of personal choice not of public practice. We can get ideas from radio, television or books; we can learn meditation at a meditation-centre and practise it at home. There is less reason to support any sort of institutional church, when we can pick and choose our beliefs from a variety of sources ourselves. Peter Clarke considers that there will be even less church-going in the future; but that religion will remain as a private thing; that seems to be the direction things are going in now.

The general message of the new religious movements is of a kind of mystical individualism. They do not talk of a God above; they say that we are all divine. They are very much based on techniques of increased self-awareness. And they often claim that all religions are saying the same thing anyway – though, of course, their own particular brand says it better. These movements do offer something the Christian churches are not seen to be giving: a stress on personal experience and self-realisation and a freedom from restrictive dogma. But the price of their privatisation of religion is that religion also becomes marginalised and thus increasingly irrelevant to society at large, and its concerns. Religion becomes like opera or stamp-collecting, a hobby for those of that inclination; its claim to truth and eternal importance has evaporated into a set of methods for feeling good.

However spectacular the rise of new religious movements in Britain, it does not reverse the general trend of decline in religious observance. Britain is, in a real sense, a secular society, and any religious beliefs and feelings there are must be fairly well hidden. There is a story that when Khrushchev, the Russian leader, met Geoffrey Fisher, the then Archbishop of Canterbury, in Moscow, he asked for some advice on how to eradicate Christian belief as effectively as had been done in Britain. That story is legendary; but it makes a telling point. Lesslie Newbigin, formerly Bishop of Madras in the Church of South India, says, in his best-selling book, *The Other Side of 1984*, 'It is significant that the only people who still cherish confidence in the future are the dissidents in each camp. The only convinced Marxists are the dissidents in the west, and the only convinced liberals are the dissidents in the east.'

I think it is true that there is a sort of disillusionment apparent in British culture, a lack of confidence in the most basic ideas which have been the foundation of our liberal culture. Our faith in science may remain intact, because it works; it produces new technical marvels every year. But our faith in the values which gave birth to science, in our ability to control the progress of science, in human reason itself, has been undermined. In a world where we might destroy ourselves totally at any moment, and where millions starve while we burn tonnes of grain, our confidence in reason evaporates. It has brought us to the brink of destruction, and our hopes of the progressive improvement of humanity through the calm application of rational principles have been shattered by two world wars and the terrible prospect of increasing violence and anarchy ahead of us. We set our hopes on human reason; and human reason is not enough to save us from power and passion, greed and envy. Deprived of the traditional Christian support that the cosmos itself is the product of supreme reason, so that human reason really is fitted to understand things as they are, human reason can easily come to seem an ephemeral and unreliable mechanism for coping with various environmental pressures. And once it is dethroned, it may be hard to find anything to put in its place, which can provide a firm basis for giving human life purpose, dignity and value, and which can give us faith to go without despair when our dreams are not realised.

The great movement of eighteenth-century thought known as the Enlightenment tended to reject religion as unduly dogmatic, as requiring acceptance of beliefs without sufficient evidence, and as holding people back in a state of submissive subservience to the whimsical tyranny of an anthropomorphic God. It rejected dogmatic and revealed religion in favour of a religion of reason. To Reason were now assigned the old prerogatives of God. It became an absolute and eternal standard by which every custom and belief was to be judged. It would inevitably lead to the establishment of a perfectly just society. It would progressively reveal all the secrets of nature, and bring in the rule of universal peace and justice. Thus, while the Enlightenment was born of Christian theism, it quickly cast off its origins and began to pursue the realisation of its great dream, the perfect society in which pure reason would rule supreme.

The dream of the Enlightenment has been shattered irrevocably by successive hammer-blows. Whereas it was once thought that reason was the measure of all things, the work of Darwin and his successors seems to show that human reason is simply a mechanism for adapting to environment, the result of a long chapter of accidents, not an organ for discovering absolute truths. Moreover, the idea that reason is a supremely impartial faculty, somehow above any particular culture, seems to have been demolished by the work of anthropologists and psychologists, who show how very culture-relative all our ideals and beliefs are, and how human reasons are very often simply rationalisations of our own social position or our own hidden desires. Further scientific study of human beings and of the brain suggests that humans are the playthings of the genes, or of unconscious forces and instinctual desires of various sorts. Reason at last comes to be seen as the slave of passion, a by-product of brain-processes which have been thrown up by accidental processes of nature.

Reason has suffered from internal dissolution, too. The Enlightenment began with the confident appeal to reason, to the impartial examination of experience and to the critical method of argument, in order to arrive at truth. But as it worked these things out, it began, inexorably and with apparent inevitability, to destroy itself. By its continued and ruthless criticism of every position of faith, it eventually undermined faith in reason itself. So it moved from the view that the use of reason would soon bring universal agreement and peace, to the much more depressing view that the human brain was probably a rather inefficient, or even pathological, accidental by-product of molecular processes, incapable of achieving even a measure of agreement, let alone absolute truth.

In twentieth-century Britain, we are the inheritors of this process of the critical self-destruction of reason. It is not only Christianity which has been weakened, but the dream of the Enlightenment, and those forms of faith which rely on it. Traditional religion had put its faith in an objective reason, in a God who had made the world in accordance with inscrutable but rational and good purposes of his own. The Enlightenment had subjectivised this idea, and put its faith in the reason of man, in the autonomy and dignity of the cognitive powers of human beings. But as investigations in the natural and human sciences progressed, encroaching materialism exorcised this last ghost from the machine of nature, and left only clockwork and the blind and ceaseless battering of little billiard-balls against each other in the emptiness of endless space. In this century, as we shall see in the next chapter, even the clockwork has gone, swallowed by quantum physics and the realisation that all theories are by-products of molecular processes in the brain. It is hardly surprising if increasing nihilism and irrationalism are characteristic of our culture. Our discovery of a secular society, the liberation from Christian faith for which Nietzsche longed and which we have largely accomplished, has not proved to be paradise. If we look deeper into the heart of our society, we can see a sort of confusion and despair there which has nothing much to do with religion; but which may have something to do with the lack of it. Bishop Newbigin says that, on his return to Britain after nearly forty years in India, the first thing to strike him about this country was the absence of hope. 'Even in the worst slums of Madras, there always seemed to be the idea that there is something better ahead. Whereas, coming back to this country, I felt that middle-aged people were just hoping to keep reasonably comfortable until they had to go to the crematorium, and many young people had no expectation of anything beyond the nuclear holocaust.' And this is not just something that could be resolved by a new political policy; it seems to be a deep malaise of spirit, profoundly reminiscent of the Biblical comment: 'Without vision, the people perish.' Dr Newbigin, too, traces the roots of this malaise back to the Enlightenment: 'The world-view we have now is the result of the Enlightenment belief that science can tell us everything about the world. And the point about it is that it excludes the idea of purpose. *I* may have purposes, but *the world* as such has no purpose; things do not have purposes. What happens then is that your world falls into two parts. One is the public world, the world of facts, to be studied objectively and dispassionately. The other is the private world of my purposes; but they just have to be my choice, my personal preference, not rooted in the nature of things. Christianity falls into the private world; so it is no longer a matter of fact, just one personal opinion among others, beyond rational debate, a pure matter of choice.'

One of the great dangers of our time in this situation is that we are facing the possibility of a blind fundamentalist conservative reaction against the Enlightenment, which could sweep away things that are enormously precious. We owe to the Enlightenment the freedom of conscience and thought which we take for granted in our society. We can never go back, as if the Enlightenment had never happened; or, worse, as though we think it ought not to have happened. But it does seem quite hard to see a way forward, to a positive but clearly post-Enlightenment view. 'The development of critical thought in the last two or three hundred years has been enormously fruitful,' Bishop Newbigin goes on. 'But it can also be deceptive.

Because you cannot criticise anything except on the basis of something you believe to be true. If you distrusted all your beliefs at the same time, you would have to go into a psychiatric hospital. We always have to start with an act of faith – that what I see is really there; that what you tell me is true; that the teacher who teaches me philosophy is competent in the subject and that I can trust him. Later I may well criticise; but faith must come first.'

Of course, the problem with that is: faith in what? 'The scientific world-view has produced immense results, both for the enlarging of our understanding of the world, and for our capacity to cope with and control it. But it has not produced a meaningful world; that seems to me to be the crucial point. Why is it that astrology is one of the most rapidly growing industries precisely in the most highly scientific cultures, like West Germany? It is because the most exhaustive analysis of the causes of things still leaves the real questions people have unanswered. If you exclude purpose from your understanding of things, and confine it to the realm of the private and subjective, then you are left in a meaningless world.'

Now, you may well say that we do have a meaningless world, and that is that. All the same, the point seems to be a good one, that if there is a meaning and purpose in the world, the techniques of science, which explicitly and intentionally rule out purpose, are not going to discover it. A different sort of approach is necessary, and if we cannot find one, our values and beliefs will seem to lack reasonable foundation. 'You cannot have values hanging in the air,' Bishop Newbigin believes. 'They have to be based on some understanding of how things are. Those of us that believe human beings do exist for a purpose, which is to enjoy God and glorify him for ever, believe that if this purpose is excluded, the real basis for human values also disappears.'

It is not surprising, then, that there has been a decline in religious observance in this century in Britain. The scientific world-view seems to exclude purpose from the universe, and thus to deprive traditional values of their basis. It privatises religion and morality and relegates them to the inner world of personal preference, thus depriving them of authority and absoluteness. It makes religious knowledge seem like a form of deviant knowledge, not to be publicly recognised and not testable by any generally shared criteria of rationality at all. At the same time, there is a general disillusionment with those very criteria of rationality which have given rise to the scientific world-view. For the methods of rational criticism seem to have destroyed, not only all the arguments for God or for absolute values, but also for any positive views at all, even a faith in reason as ultimately trustworthy. When it is probed more deeply, even the scientific world-view crumbles, exposed as just one more ideology among others; and this leads to a virtually complete nihilism about beliefs. So the decline of Christianity in Britain seems to be part of a wider decline of belief in any set of values or ideals at all. And this is allied with a general loss of social confidence, the collapse of a coherent and common basis of national life. The churches, like the nation as a whole, are confused about their role and image in the world. Like the nation, they sometimes seem to be perpetually apologising for still tentatively holding onto beliefs that they once proclaimed with confident pride. The outlook seems bleak.

Can this decline of religious belief be reversed? Or should it be? Not only do I think it can and should be; I believe the reverse has begun, and that is what I propose to argue in this book. The social scene is indeed depressing; but that is because it reflects the ideas of the recent, but already outdated, past. A whole new set of ideas exists, and is fomenting just beneath the surface. The formation of a fully post-Enlightenment philosophy is in progress which in no way rejects the critical or scientific methods, but which is able to place them in a fuller and more positive perspective. It may be hard for the churches or for society at large to absorb this revolution in thought, but it must do so, whether soon or late.

In the following chapters, I shall try to sketch this process in the sciences, in metaphysics and ethical thought, in the discipline of theology itself, and in the encounter of diverse religious and cultural traditions. I would like to try to convey something of the intellectual excitement and challenge of this quiet revolution in thought, and to show how Christian faith finds itself involved at the very growing-point of new and creative developments. The import of this first chapter is that we are, in Britain, indeed in a cultural crisis, hardly for the first time in our history. Our apologetic and sceptical attitudes to religion reflect this fact. But beneath the surface, new views and attitudes are being formed. And it is in these, not in the number of people who go to churches, that we may seek to measure the true state of Christian belief in Britain today, and its prospects for the future.

Chapter Two
THE PHANTOM BATTLE

'Chance alone is at the source of every innovation . . . pure chance, absolutely free but blind, at the very root of the stupendous edifice of evolution; this central concept of modern biology . . . is today the sole conceivable hypothesis, the only one compatible with observed and tested facts', wrote the French biologist, Jacques Monod, in a recent book, *Chance and Necessity*. His words seem to echo the thought, often expressed, that there is a war between science and religious faith. Science, as Monod expresses it from his viewpoint as a biologist, sees the world as a product of pure chance, without purpose or design, moving by blind laws to a totally accidental end; whereas religion sees the world as created for a purpose by a personal and good God. These two views are completely opposed; so science and religion are bound to be enemies.

That is a fairly widespread perception of how modern science undermines and opposes Christian faith; and it is no doubt one main reason why people are hesitant about claiming truth for Christian ideas about God's creation and purpose. But is it an accurate perception? Does it really reflect the state of modern science? Or is it an outdated piece of anti-religious dogma? It must be admitted that Monod was being consciously provocative in putting his point as bluntly as he did. A more measured statement of the same general view is given by Richard Dawkins, also a biologist, at Oxford University. He is the author of *The Blind Watchmaker*, which, he says, 'is an attempt to explain Darwin's theory of natural selection as it plays its role as, in a sense, replacing God in our world-view.'

Dawkins rejects the view that there is any ultimate purpose in the universe. 'However, when a biologist looks at particular organs or organisms, an eye or a brain, what he sees is a machine which has every indication of being designed for a purpose. In that sense, living things quite obviously do have a purpose. But natural selection manages to explain how they came into being without there being an ultimate purpose. There is admittedly a strain between the thought of blind chance and design. For living beings are not only designed; they are supremely well designed, beautifully designed and far more complicated than any man-made machine. But what is so magnificent about Darwinian explanation is that it does manage to show how blind forces of physics could, given enough time, build up these highly complicated machines.'

Darwin's theory, or at least the updated form of it which takes into account recent advances in genetics, of which Darwin knew virtually nothing, has two main features. First, mutations happen in the genetic material at random, changing the character of new individuals, sometimes favourably but often unfavourably. Second, some individuals are selected by the environment for survival. That is to say, some of them are able to survive better and reproduce more prodigally, because of the quite fortuitous fact that they are slightly better suited to their environment than their competitors. So, over a very long period of time, the combination of random mutation and selection by environment brings about the survival of some species and the elimination of others. On the whole, one finds that more complex, adaptable and perceptive organisms survive and reproduce better. So there seems to be a 'selection' of such individuals. In reality, however, nothing is needed to account for the whole process of evolution than those two basic factors of mutation and environmental selection, neither of which is purposive, or needs to use the notion of purpose.

For Dawkins, the theory of natural selection is entirely sufficient to explain how living things have evolved, even though they give every appearance of being superbly designed. 'I do not think it would be possible to *rule out* a designing God,' he says, 'but natural selection does make God superfluous. My own view is that where something is both superfluous and exceedingly complicated and therefore improbable in its own right, we are better off being positively sceptical about it.' Belief in God is not *incompatible* with natural selection: 'The mere fact that so many distinguished biologists are religious should be enough to disprove that hypothesis. But the whole point about natural selection is that it manages to take extreme simplicity as its starting point and give rise to extreme complexity at its finishing point. It is very difficult to understand how very complicated things happen. Darwinism succeeds in doing that, whereas God would be very complicated, and would himself need explaining.'

Obviously, then, there are distinguished biologists who think that natural selection gives an adequate explanation for the existence of life on earth. But that opinion is highly disputable – other biologists, like W. H. Thorpe or Sir Alister Hardy, do not think that natural selection can produce the goods in the time available. Some, including Francis Crick, one of the discoverers of the molecular structure of DNA, the basic substance which carries the genetic code, and so enables organisms to replicate themselves, have been led to postulate that life must have come to the earth from outer space. Random selection alone could not have produced the life we see around us in the lifetime of the earth. Other scientists find it so highly improbable that blind chance alone would produce Dawkins' 'supremely well designed' machines that they argue that it would be more reasonable to see purpose as guiding the process towards the existence of sentient, rational beings. Paul Davies, Professor of Mathematical Physics at the University of Newcastle, puts the point in this way: 'I would look for a meaning in the laws of physics themselves. They make use of randomness in some way; but there is no inconsistency between that and saying that the fundamental laws of physics themselves have had to be set up in a rather precise way. We must distinguish between chance in the development of things and chance in the laws themselves. It seems to me that the laws are in no sense chancy, though they embody chance as part of their mechanism.'

Davies' idea is not that God would have to keep intervening, to produce better designed organisms; but that something very like God is necessary to explain how the laws of chance themselves come to be so precisely balanced as they have to be, to allow natural selection to produce the effects it does. That suggests that natural selection, though it may work within its own limits, is not in fact a sufficient explanation of how life has evolved. It leaves the structure of the laws themselves entirely unexplained.

Even within the realm of biology, though, there are areas where natural selection seems to run up against theoretical limitations. As we have seen, on that theory, all we basically need to appeal to are chemical mistakes in the reproduction of gene-codes. Some of these flourish better than others in their environments; and so they reproduce more effectively. It is as simple as that – mistakes in chemistry and a (sometimes) fortuitous survival capacity in the environment. All that is needed to explain the genesis of life on earth as we have it today is some slightly inefficient gene-reproducing mechanism in the chemistry of the body and sufficient time for many combinations to occur.

That this concatenation of accidents gave rise to the appearance of 'supremely designed' machines seems more extraordinary than ever; and further major difficulties remain. Professor Davies again: 'I cannot see how purely factory-line, mechanistic processes at the molecular level are ever going to provide explanations for things like the development of the embryo or the existence of structure and form on a large scale. It always seems to me a rather paradoxical thing that some sort of controlling mechanism at the molecular level can organise something like an embryo over the size of several centimetres. Trying to explain how there can exist an overall plan for an organism, on a large scale, in terms of something controlled at the molecular level, seems to me to be a very difficult problem. As a physicist, I am very deeply baffled by these attempts to explain in this Newtonian, mechanistic, reductionist way these holistic and collective aspects of developmental biology.'

So deep mysteries remain in biology; and while no one wishes to bring God in as the solution of problems as yet unsolved, this does place a large question-mark against any attempt to say that natural selection alone gives a sufficient explanation of the development of life. It is worth remembering that when we call a genetic mutation random, we really mean that we cannot assign a particular cause for its happening thus, and not otherwise. It is a statement of ignorance, not of knowledge. There is no way in which we could exclude purpose from the sorts of molecular changes that occur in nature, even though natural selection could be a major part of the mechanism involved. In fact, Richard Dawkins confesses that something odd begins to happen once human beings have evolved, which natural selection alone cannot account for: 'Darwin's theory is not a sufficient explanation for culture, civilisation, art, mathematics, and many aspects of life around us. What Darwin's theory does is to explain how brains came into being. Once you have brains of a sufficient complexity there is the possibility of those brains taking off and developing a new kind of evolution – things which have no direct Darwinian explanation. The Darwinian world-view provides the basic raw material; I would not wish to find a Darwinian explanation of why, for instance, we should value truth. I feel it as a personal imperative.'

This must be regarded as a very significant concession. Human beings are, after all, animals; and if new principles of explanation are required for their behaviour, it is very difficult to suppose that those principles were not present in any form in the development of the processes which led, with apparent inevitability, to their existence. Would it not be a highly plausible supposition that the raw material was developed precisely in order to allow this new form of evolution to come into being? Well, as Dawkins says, you could not rule that out. So it seems that even the non-theistic biologists are not claiming, really, that God is impossible, or that his existence would be quite pointless (since this would *ensure* that things evolved very largely in the way they have; and nothing else we can think of would). It is just that Dawkins finds him superfluous, and a bit messy and complicated.

We shall return to the question of whether God is complex in Chapter Three. But is he really superfluous? Dawkins says, 'My view, if you think about its aesthetic or even moral connotations, is a bleak and cold one. If you wanted to try to draw ethical principles out of it I think you would probably fail. To the extent that you would succeed, they might be rather nasty principles.' This cannot be dismissed as an unimportant point, either. It is often said that you must not judge the truth of a theory by its ethical consequences. But if you find that its consequences are at odds with beliefs and imperatives you deeply hold, that these imperatives would be undermined if you accepted the theory, then this is one good argument that the theory is false. It is not false just because you do not like it; but if a very general theory conflicts with many particular beliefs, that should cause you at least to examine the theory very carefully. You might be justifiably more certain of your beliefs than you are that the theory of natural selection is *sufficient* to exclude purpose from the universe. In the previous chapter, Bishop Newbigin claimed that it was the elimination of purpose from the universe which had given rise to a widespread sense of despair and meaninglessness; and Dawkins is virtually admitting as much himself, though he prefers the heroic course of just facing up to the harsh truth. If it turns out that biology cannot exclude purpose; and that, even on those

Darwinian principles which it uses within its proper limits, the way things are is quite consistent with purpose, then we are able to search for a purpose and meaning in the world which might put our human life and concerns in a wider perspective – and not such a bleak one as Dawkins himself sees.

David Bartholomew is Professor of Mathematical Statistics at the London School of Economics. He admits that for some years the views of respected biologists like Monod that the existence of chance rules out ideas of purpose in the universe, raised intellectual difficulties for him. But in fact this is not so; and it is David Bartholomew's own subject, mathematical statistics, which shows that it is not so. 'We have become accustomed, since Newton, to think of the world as a vast well-oiled machine. And if chance plays a leading role in the scheme of things, then it appears at first sight to eliminate the connecting-rods of purpose. But we need to think, in a rather more fundamental way than we have often done, about what chance is and how things happen as a result of chance. Chance has to do with unpredictability, uncertainty, randomness – these are all words we may use to convey something of the flavour of the idea. Contemporary physicists would believe that there is some fundamental chance built into the universe, in sub-atomic processes. But that does not rule out scientific laws. The laws that Newton and others taught us are still operational, even if they are good working approximations rather than exactly predictable processes. Some of these laws are simply due to the effect of large numbers, the aggregate effect of large numbers of things. Thus if I hold up a piece of paper it stays upright because the particles on each side are roughly equal in number. In somewhat the same way, where you have a very large aggregate of chance events you may well get purpose and order.'

So you can get a very large number of events at the sub-atomic level which are random and unpredictable in detail. But when that large number is taken as a whole, we may be able to predict the outcome with a very high degree of probability. Maybe a good analogy would be with a crowd at a football match. We could never predict what each person will do, as an individual; perhaps each one is free and unpredictable. Yet we can predict the behaviour of the crowd as a whole – when it will disperse, for instance – almost certainly. Random events can build up into sequences the outcome of which is pretty certain.

So it may be that: 'Each genetic mutation in the process of

evolution is random. But a very large number of such mutations over a very long period of time may inevitably in the end lead to some highly organised form of life, such as ourselves.' Though individual events taken in isolation appear random – that is, unpredictable from knowledge of previous states of those events – the general structure of the physical environment which determines the changes that are selected for survival, can lead to a virtually inevitable overall goal. Thus the whole structure may well be purposive; but the way that purpose works out is largely through random, or what appear to us to be random, changes. David Bartholmew suggests a simple analogy: 'A very simple example is that of a person at the North Pole who wants to get to the South Pole. He has a choice of directions; and he may choose any one at random. But, whichever one he takes, he will get to the South Pole eventually.'

We can see, then, how Monod has over-stated his case. God could have so set up the universe that it is bound to reach the goal he has set for it, even though it does so by means of many random or indeterminate fluctuations. Mathematically, this can be demonstrated quite convincingly. But of course it leaves us with the problem of why God would want to leave so much to chance, along the way. What point is there in building randomness into the structure of things? David Bartholomew thinks that this rather new view of the universe, in which chance plays a much more prominent role than it did in Newton's universe, makes the Christian view of things more rather than less plausible.

'Take the problem of evil, for instance, which is perhaps the biggest stumbling block that the Christian has to cope with. We are not required to believe that every single act, every deformed baby that is born, is a direct act of God; and that therefore some explanation must be found, whether it is the sin of parents or whatever. In a random universe some things are bound to go wrong; that is the inevitable price to be paid for a universe in which there is real freedom.' If we are to be really free and morally responsible, then there has to be a measure of randomness and uncertainty in the world. Freedom is not the same as uncertainty at all. But if everything was completely determined from the beginning, then real freedom could not exist. So indeterminacy is one necessary condition of freedom. A theist can plausibly argue that a universe with really free beings in it realises distinctive sorts of values that could not exist in an unfree universe. We can hardly imagine what an existence would be like without risk, challenge, surprise, excitement – and thus without danger, defeat and despair, sometimes. Perhaps, then, if beings like us are worth creating at all, they could only exist in a partly indeterminate universe. If so, we have to take the consequence that not all dangers and sufferings can be avoided. It is, to put it crudely, often just the luck of the draw.

I do not suppose that this argument will carry conviction for everyone; certainly not without a lot of further thought. But it is possible to see how a partly random universe may be necessary to the production of certain kinds of good. Such a universe may even be a necessary expression of the nature of the creator himself. And if the events in it, however terrible or haphazard they may seem, can be brought to some sort of fulfilment beyond this linear time, in God, then one might see how the creator could be called 'good' – not in the sense that he never causes harm (that would be demonstrably false); but in the sense that he brings value even out of the chance and evil that seem to be necessarily involved in the creation of free creatures.

Even if one finds it hard to call such a creator 'good', however, David Bartholomew's point at least shows that chance is quite compatible with purpose; and that chance is even necessary to the realisation of certain kinds of purpose. So it is quite possible to accept Darwin's view of evolution, or something rather like it, and also believe there is a purpose in the universe. Bartholomew concludes: 'I think this enables us to give a clearer and perhaps more coherent account of why the universe should be the way it is. I would say that science actually helps religious belief today. It certainly destroys some people's beliefs; but that may be a good thing. It gives us a very much larger picture of the world. We can see it as a greater, more sophisticated, more elaborate structure than we might otherwise have imagined. Scientific understanding can enrich faith and enlarge it.'

There is obviously not much trace of a great animosity between science and religion here. Professor Bartholomew did say that scientific advances can create difficulties for our understanding of how the world is related to God. That is hardly surprising; for each time science advances to a new view, we have to readjust our whole perception of things to take account of it. But the end result can be an enrichment and enlargement of faith, or of the way we understand the nature of the world, as showing the purpose of God.

One of the most important insights of modern science is that there is not just one level of explanation to which all others can be reduced. That was a dream of the very early nineteenth century, and it was known as the programme of scientific reductionism. It was hoped that all the sciences could be reduced to one basic level, perhaps that of physics. This has not proved to be possible. As we shall see a little later, physicists no longer adopt a 'building-block' view of the physical universe, so that its complex wholes can be fully explained in terms of the properties of their parts. On the contrary, the nature of the parts turns out to be an abstraction which will depend partly on the nature of the wholes within which they exist. The lowest level of explanation turns out to be an abstraction from the rich complexity of the whole. Far from explaining everything, it gives a very skeletal outline of some rather abstract properties, and leaves the rest wholly untouched.

It is now widely recognised that scientists work with a world which operates at many levels of interpretation, each of them valid in its own terms, but none of them exhaustively describing the whole. Pehaps it is biologists, these days, who still tend to retain something of that old dream, long given up by physics. But most biologists realise that we need to take a much more open and plural approach to the complex reality of the physical universe.

In the words of Dr Arthur Peacocke, a biologist who is Director of the Ramsey Institute at Oxford University: 'There are various levels of complexity in the world, each with its own level of interpretation. The level, which I am more familiar with, of atoms and molecules, going up to the more complex systems of biology, is only one of many. The level of chemistry, of biochemistry, physiology, or the whole organism considered as part of some ecosystem – each of these has its own interpretation at its own level and is real at its own level. Each requires special methods of investigation, appropriate to that level of complexity. You find that new conceptions are developed, appropriate to each level; and they are often not, in principle, reducible to conceptions that apply at lower levels. For instance, even though complex wholes are made up of the bits about which physics and chemistry write, there are concepts which are peculiar to biology, and can in no way be translated into concepts of physics or chemistry. So if we have a hierarchy of levels of complexity in the natural world, we should not be surprised that at the level of the most complex bit of matter in the universe – the human brain and body – new concepts will be necessary to explain what is going on at the level of personal life and history. They will not be reducible even to the concepts of sociology, let alone biochemistry or physics.'

If a materialist is a person who holds that there is just one world, but that it operates at many levels of complexity, the highest of which requires us to use such concepts as those of responsibility, intention and rationality, then materialism is quite harmless, and is just an unusual word for what we all believe. It is certainly compatible with the Christian view that human beings are fully psycho-physical organisms, truly belonging to the material world but at a very high, indeed unique level of complexity. Why, then, should it sometimes be thought that sciences like biology somehow threaten to reduce human beings to nothing but bundles of macro-molecules? Dr Peacocke suggests that it is something to do with the extraordinary explosion of biology in the last thirty years. This has included a new understanding of mechanisms of heredity and many areas of human behaviour which were totally opaque at the beginning of the century. So it is not surprising that biologists have a great sense of confidence in their subject, and sometimes think they can make a take-over bid for the rest of human knowledge. But patently, even socio-biology does not go very far towards explaining such things as moral impera-tives or many other areas which biology cannot touch at all. We can gratefully accept the explanatory theories of biology within its proper sphere of experimental study; but gently resist the grander claim that these theories tell us all we need to know about human nature and behaviour.

This is not to say that the tremendous advances in the sciences since the sixteenth century leave religious faith quite untouched. But Christianity, in Dr Peacocke's words, 'has been in continuous dialogue with the sciences from the first; and it has faced up to the intellectual challenges in a way which enriches understanding of the creator.' Perhaps the first great challenge was that represented in most people's minds by Galileo – the discovery that the earth was not the centre of the universe, but, as we later came to see, on the edge of a small galaxy. Human beings are not the purpose of the universe – or it is most unlikely that they are. Even evolution on the surface of this planet does not really look like a process which is all directed just to produce us. It looks much more like a random exploration on the part of the natural world to develop all the forms that are potential within its structure. Built into the system, however, is this potentiality for producing complex sensitive organisms like us. This is certainly not a man-centred view of things; but it enables us to see much more of the immense power and wisdom of the creator of the whole universe. Why should human beings be the centre of his purposes, after all? Christianity met the first challenge by recovering the insight that it is God who is the centre of all things, not man.

This should have been much easier than it was; for Thomas Aquinas, in the thirteenth century, had clearly formulated the view that the existence of human beings, and indeed of the whole universe, makes no essential difference to God. God himself, Aquinas said, is already perfect and changeless. He cannot really be affected by anything that happens in creation. Thus, in a real sense, whatever humans do is irrelevant to God. Our task is not to help God to be happier, but simply to see him for what he is, and respond with that worship which is our natural response to perfection. This is far from being a man-centred view of things. Only God matters; and humanity's happiness lies in coming to know God. Given that the church had already officially adopted this view by the time of Galileo, it should have had no difficulty in accepting his theories. The ecclesiastical resistance was probably more due to reliance on the authority of Aristotle than to any especially theological considerations. So that first challenge was not too hard to meet.

The second challenge was Newton's radically new perception that the whole universe is governed by mathematically simple laws; not by direct spirit-guidance and activity. After that, God could no longer be thought of as directly deciding to hurl every bolt of lightning. This challenge, in turn, was met by the recognition that the laws of nature, in their beauty and elegance, show a supremely rational ordering of the universe. This is quite compatible with the existence of a personal God who guides the universe to goals of his own. Indeed, Isaac Newton was himself a firm believer in God, and regarded his own work as inspired by the search for those rational principles of order which he believed an all-wise God must have placed within his universe. Dr Peacocke again: 'The sciences show us a world in which things are interconnected; processes at one level manifest themselves in events at other levels. There is a continuous web of interconnections across space and through time, in the development of the cosmos. Its rationality, its order and its beauty, have in many of us, who are scientists, evoked such a sense of wonder that we think it can only be rendered comprehensible by postulating some supra-mind from which it derives its being.'

Again, science increases our sense of the greatness of God. All it demolishes are some rather simplistic ideas, like God walking on the mountain-tops, riding on the clouds, hurling thunderbolts or sending plagues and locusts. Many of these were undoubtedly meant metaphorically anyway – the Biblical writers did not really think God had hands and feet, though he could appear in visions in human form. Others are a more serious problem, since they do regard God as directly acting to cause rain or drought. Opinions differ among theologians as to how to treat such Biblical doctrines. Some would say they must just be dropped, and we must ascribe everything that happens to natural causality. However, it seems possible to say that God wills most events to occur in accordance with the laws of regularity he himself has instituted. But at other times he acts concurrently with those laws – that is to say, without breaking them, he uses them to express purposes of his own, and directs them in accordance with his intentions (rather as we do, when we use the laws of mechanics to put billiard balls in pockets). And again, he may very occasionally, and for very special purposes, cause objects to act beyond their natural powers altogether. These would be miracles; and there seems to be no reason why science as such should exclude them. For science deals precisely with the general regularities of things. And if a miracle is an irregularity, brought about by God as a fairly unique event to be a sort of transfiguration of the physical to disclose its spiritual foundation, a temporal shadow cast by the light of eternity, then science has nothing to say either for or against it. Thus we can say that Newton's new perception of the universe did drive out the idea of continual and arbitrary divine activity, causing things to happen by mere whim, as it were. But it still allows both the concurrent actions of God in and through the events of nature, and the occasional miraculous action of God for special purposes of his own. It does not attack belief in God itself; and in fact can be seen, as Newton saw it, as a reflection of God's wisdom and faithfulness.

The third challenge was Darwin's theory of evolution by natural selection. At first this seemed to remove purpose from human evolution but, as we have seen, it does not in fact do that. It does, however, lead us to adopt quite a new view of the origin of human life, which had never been held at any time before in human history. We can see the process of evolution on this planet as a gradual developing of new capacities and powers out of simpler elements, in an orderly and continuous way, and yet in a way which allows for many variations and creative explorations of potential. Chance has a part to play in the evolution of the world, in a way which Newtonian science did not envisage. We can now take it as an established scientific view that self-conscious human subjects have evolved naturally out of simpler forms of existence over a fairly long period of time. This evolutionary view requires us to make many adjustments in traditional Christian thinking. All the same, it is quite compatible with the Christian doctrines of creation and of a divine providence, directing all created things towards realising some set of purposes.

Like Professor Bartholomew, Dr Peacocke sees the twentieth-century revolution in physics, following the work of Faraday and Einstein, not as a challenge to religious belief, but as positively helping to reintegrate the scientific and religious world-views. The Einstein view sees the universe as a set of overlapping fields of energy-interaction in a unified space-time, so interconnected that every event seems to affect each other event in some respect, with the effect that the whole forms a complex and integrated unity. In what way can we think of God as interacting with such a universe? The new physics suggests a model which is surprisingly like some very ancient Christian ideas of God, though it has perhaps been forgotten by many Christians. 'I think we have to see the world,' says Dr Peacocke, 'not as if God is outside the universe, like an engineer who has made a machine and is standing by, watching it running. We have to see the world as in some sense *within* God. God is the reality which is in, through and above all things; in which the world is, if you like, embedded. There is no part of the universe from which God is absent; he expresses himself in, with and under it, to use a classical phrase.'

The machine-model of the universe needs to be replaced by an organic model, in which the nature of the parts is only truly seen when their function within the whole is seen. The Newtonian picture was of relatively self-contained little atoms banging around in absolute space and time. The new picture is of a total field of interconnected energy-patterns, within which human interaction and perception can carve out particular aspects for investigation. The stress is on totality and integration; it is, we might say, a *Gestalt* view of things, not a building-block view. And on this picture, God is no longer the designer of the perfect machine. He is more like the most inclusive, highest level of interpretation of the universe as a whole, in terms of which alone it can be adequately understood in its order and purpose and meaning.

Dr Peacocke draws an analogy with music. 'The development of a piece of music is the composer expressing his inner character as creator. I think this helps to see how the world is *in itself* God's self-expressive action. He is the total reality which surrounds the world, in which it is embedded; so the sciences unveil the creative expression of God, who is the highest and most inclusive level of reality.' Another analogy might be with our own bodies. They are no doubt explicable in terms of physiology, physics and chemistry. Yet we express ourselves in and through them; and while at one level the sciences can explain what is going on in our bodies, at another level, at the level of intention and meaning and self-awareness, we need another sort of description and explanation. So we can say, here is the physical universe which the sciences tell us about. But if we ask what meanings we can discern in that world, then we may look to those traditions of interpretation, in the great religions, of what God has been saying in the world and in history. It seems quite possible that certain clusters of unique events may express the nature of God in ways which cannot be captured by the generalised laws of some specific science.

On this sort of account, religious claims to revelation go beyond the sciences, being alleged discernments of the intentions of God in the universe, as expressed in unique, personal and historical events. But they are dealing with the same reality as the sciences, with the same world of which the sciences give quite adequate accounts at their own appropriate level of interpretation. So the battle between science and religion turns out to be a sort of phantom battle between scientists who over-generalised their favourite explanatory models to try to cover absolutely everything, and religious believers who thought that the Bible could give correct answers to the problems of physics. It was a battle between a very old-fashioned and imperialistic view of science and an equally old-fashioned and imperialistic view of religion. Of course I do not mean to imply that scientists are all turning to Christianity suddenly, though a great many leading scientists are Christians. But there has been a noticeable change of climate since the early years of this century, when it was often assumed that reputable scientists had to be materialists, to the present day, when classical materialism is virtually defunct, except among some unrepentant biologists. The tide of opinion has certainly turned in this whole area, and the new physics often finds itself joining hands with religion in a quest for truth and beauty and the meaning of existence, in a quest for the ultimate explanation of things.

'I am the kind of person who wants an explanation for the way that things are and the way they happen. That is the fundamental drive of all science. I feel that there must be an ultimate explanation for how things are. So I cannot conceive of a godless universe. It is always more rational to seek for an explanation than not to. I would see a curiosity about the world in general and the way it works as basic; I have a desire to use all the tools available, scientific or otherwise, to ask questions and probe further back and to find out how it works.' Professor Bartholomew, speaking as a mathematical statistician, reveals a deep kinship between science and religion insofar as they both seek to understand why the world is the way it is. It is a sheer travesty of religion to pretend that it propounds some unthinking and dogmatic answers to all our questions and so puts a stop to all respectable enquiry. On the contrary, one of the main sources of religion is the desire to understand. Other sources are the search for meaning in human life, the experience of encounter with a higher self or will, and a sense of being confronted by a moral claim. But it is perhaps the quest for explanation, and the thought that the world is capable of rational explanation, which has led to the rise of science in the West. Some religious institutions and individuals did for a time oppose thinkers like Galileo and Darwin, preferring reliance on authority to the search for real understanding. Yet the underlying urge to understand and explain the world is common to a religion which believes in a wise and rational creator God and to the scientific enterprise. In fact, the convergence between physics and religion is quite extraordinary in recent years. Paul Davies, for instance, has written a book entitled *God and the New Physics*. This may seem a very unusual thing for a professor of physics to do, since it is not a book about religion, but just about physics. How, then, can God come into it? 'The job of the theoretical physicist is to examine the laws of physics at their most fundamental level. I found myself working in all sorts of areas of enquiry such as "How did the universe come into existence?" and "How will it end?", "What are the ultimate constituents of matter?", "What is the relationship between mind and matter?" – questions which for centuries had really remained within the province of religion or philosophy. What I was interested in was that, probably only in the last few decades, physics in particular, but science in general, has been able to address these questions too. Although we may not have complete answers, at least we are on the road to answering some of these deep questions. So, perhaps unexpectedly, physics now finds itself working in areas which formerly were the province of religion, and actually coming up with some answers. This fascinated me; and I thought maybe the time had come to take a good hard look at how some of the traditional answers of theology shape up given today's understanding of physics; that is how I came to write the book.'

Professor Davies is not a religious believer 'in any conventional sense. I don't go to church, or pray or anything of that sort. I was brought up as a Christian, and I think I subscribe to general Christian values, but I don't follow any sort of formal worship. Indeed, I'm a little bit sceptical of any form of institutional religion. I'm one of these people who believes that there is more to the world than meets the eye, that there is some meaning behind existence; but I prefer to approach that meaning through my scientific work, not through any type of collective worship.'

Here is a view of physics as itself a sort of worship, as an approach to the meaning of being, and one which evinces plenty of reverence and awe. The reason why Davies does not worship God in a more conventional way becomes clearer when one explores further how he views God: 'The physicist has learned that he must consider time as part of the physical universe. The age-old problem about whether God is within time or in some sense outside of time resurfaces with a vengeance when one comes to consider such things as the Big Bang theory, for which time literally begins with the Big Bang. In other words, the modern physicist approaches the question of the origin of the universe as being not only the origin of matter, but of space and time as well. So if we wish to consider God as creating the universe, then he has to be outside of time. The physicist can tell us that time is part of the physical world; so if we wish to approach a God who is in some generalised sense a person, a being who could communicate, think, act in some way, these are all temporal attributes; and if we wish to have a God of that sort, we would have to have him within the universe, in which case we cannot regard him as creator. If we want a God with whom we can have any sort of personal relationship, it has to be a temporal God. If we want a God who is going to be responsible for creating the totality of the physical world, then he has to be a God outside of time. I think there is a fundamental conflict between these two.'

Professor Davies' view is not really very helpful to the ordinary believer, then. But we must remember that, strange as it may seem, the traditional Christian view, as stated by Thomas Aquinas, is that God is outside time; and that when we relate to God in personal ways, in prayer and so on, we are thinking of God metaphorically, or, as it is usually put, analogically. Davies is not so far away from the orthodox Christian as he thinks. And he reacts strongly against Richard Dawkins' suggestion, referred to earlier in this chapter, that the postulate of God is totally superfluous, and that it would be much simpler just to stop with the basic laws of the universe. 'I completely disagree with this position. It seems to me, when one looks very carefully at the way in which the laws of physics have been set up, as it were, there are so many remarkable and apparently contrived features about the physical universe, I find it impossible to accept all of this as a brute fact.' It is possible to calculate mathematically just how closely the laws of physics have to be 'fine-tuned' in order that we, as thinking, conscious individuals, can be present at all. Life of any conceivable sort requires rather delicate and special conditions in the universe. These conditions we have absolutely no right to expect on *a priori* grounds. Thus we find ourselves living in a universe that almost seems, in some sense, to have been designed for habitation. Science cannot prove that it is so designed. If we are talking about something which is supernatural, which lies behind this or which gives the physical world a meaning, that lies inevitably beyond science. What science can do is to establish whether or not there is anything terribly remarkable about the world we live in. Professor Davies says, 'Modern physics has shown that there is something truly extraordinary about the way the laws of physics fit together, the way the universe has been put together. It is not just any old universe; it is a very very special, fine-tuned arrangement of things.'

Just when philosophers had thought that the argument from design was gone for ever, the physicist brings it back again. One might try the following analogy: if you shuffle a pack of cards, you may deal them and find that all the cards come out in proper order, suit by suit. That would be extraordinary, but it is just possible, once in a lifetime. But if it happened time after time, we would say, 'This is too extraordinary to be chance; the deck has been fixed.' So, the structure of physical laws show a great number of extraordinary balances and correspondences, which are necessary if things like us are ever to exist. It is that extraordinariness which makes it highly probable that, as Professor Davies puts it, 'something is going on'.

Just what is going on, though, is highly mysterious. The clockwork universe that Newton constructed, with its solid little atoms bouncing off one another, has now been demolished. The new physics has completely swept aside a lot of the cosy old intuitive notions that people carry around about the nature of matter. In particular, the apparent solidity of matter has been undermined. Quantum physics deals with the atom and its constituents, and as one probes smaller and smaller distances, the concrete matter of our senses dissolves away into a sort of ghostly mêlée of vibrating energy-patterns. It seems that there is virtually no substance there at all. It turns out to be completely impossible to ascribe a complete set of physical attributes to an object like an electron. If you want to think of an electron as like a tiny billiard-ball, circling in orbit around a central nucleus, at the least you feel it ought to be somewhere, and it ought to be moving in some way, along a precisely defined trajectory. But it turns out that, according to Heisenberg's Principle of Indeterminacy, an electron simply cannot have both a position and a motion at the same time. In other words, we cannot really think of an electron as a thing, independently existing in its own right, whether we observe it or not. The whole idea of 'constituents' of things becomes very difficult. In some sense we know that the atom is made up of smaller particles. The so-called quarks, which are supposedly the building-blocks of all nuclear material, and the electrons and some other particles that are similar make up what we call matter. But when we try to grab hold of these little objects, we find that they behave in a very peculiar fashion. We cannot think of the world as made up of these little objects in the same way that a house is made up of bricks, the whole just being the sum of its parts.

That was the view sometimes called 'mechanistic material-ism', of which Professor Davies roundly declares: 'As far as physics is concerned, mechanistic materialism has been dead for fifty years. It is rather curious that in molecular biology this old-fashioned reductionism and mechanism still thrives, on the physics of the nineteenth century. There is a completely fresh point of view, which is sweeping through the physics community, partly because of the lessons of quantum physics. You simply cannot consider the universe as a clockwork mechanism, rigidly ticking over some predetermined pathway towards a final destiny. That idea collapsed in the nineteen twenties. There has been much more emphasis in recent years on processes which are in some sense collective or holistic or which are unpredictable even without quantum effects, effects which are so sensitive to initial conditions that it is simply not possible to predict how they will behave. In other words, there is a growing interest among physicists and other physical scientists in self-organising systems where one has to look at the totality, and not just at individual bits and pieces. This is still very much a new subject; it is still wide open. But the old-fashioned paradigm of a clockwork universe slavishly unfol-ding according to the laws of cause and effect really has been demolished.'

There are two important points here. First, the old material-ism has gone for ever. The solid little building-blocks have dis-solved into vibrating energy-patterns. As the famous physicist Max Born put it in 1946: 'We are not justified in concluding that the "thing" under examination can actually be described as a particle in the usual sense of the term' (*Atomic Physics*). Elec-trons are like particles guided by probability-waves, and prob-ability-waves do not, in any straightforward sense, exist.

Werner Heisenberg, one of the founders of quantum physics, said, 'All we can give as a description is a probability-function . . . we are concerned with a possibility of existing or with a tendency to exist.' So particles have lost their concrete qualities and even their individuality: they have become mathematical structures, or unpicturable realities partially mapped by such structures. In such a world, we can no longer say that we can account for everything that happens by knowing all the properties of the basic building-blocks of matter; we have lost those blocks. And second, we may have to use new principles of explanation to understand the universe, scarcely worked out as yet – what Davies calls holistic principles, of structure and order, in which we explain the behaviour of the parts in terms of their whole context, and not the other way round. This is again a major blow for classical materialism, as it means we may only finally be able to say what matter is when we see the whole context within which it exists. In a word, the universe is now perceived by physics to be more intelligible and mind-like and unitary than made up of many independent, solid, inert and accidentally related atoms.

A recent book by Fritjof Capra, an Austrian physicist, attempts to spell out something of the nature of matter as contemporary physicists see it. He traces what he finds to be a remarkable similarity between the physicists' world-view and the thought-forms of Eastern mysticism, and says, 'The philosophy of mystical traditions provides the most consistent philosophical background to our modern scientific theories.' It is perhaps a pity that Capra shows virtually no knowledge of mystical traditions within Christianity, or of the orthodox theologies which place a much greater stress on intuitive wisdom and poetic insight than some of the later more rationalistic Christian systems. So he ignores the Christian dimension altogether. Nevertheless, his work does show how many physicists now work with a view of the world very different from that of classical materialism, and more sympathetic to philosophies which see the basis of matter itself as fundamentally mind-like and intelligible. The physical basis of reality is much stranger than we thought. It makes very good sense to see this whole physical universe, in Dr Peacocke's phrase, as 'embedded' within a wider supra-temporal reality of God; that is, a being of wisdom, intelligence and purpose, which gives ultimate meaning to the way things are.

Although Professor Davies feels that physics now provides a more secure route to the God which traditional theology sought, his view is still rather too deistic for the average religious believer. As he says, he does not worship or pray, or regard God as personal in any way. He thinks the universe has got a meaning; but he does not think we need any sort of interventionist God to keep it running smoothly. In a sense, that is unobjectionable to the religious believer. God does not need to keep interfering in order to keep the universe running. But on the other hand, it is rather odd to say that the ultimate basis of reality is spiritual and intelligible, that it may well have meaning and purpose; but that it has no particular effects in the physical world at all. It is only reasonable to think that some particular events in the material universe will be effected by the being of God, so that they would not have been what they are except for the presence and purpose of God. God will have particular effects on the universe; but perhaps we should not expect the sciences themselves to be able to detect these. There are, after all, some obvious differences between scientific and religious questions.

Professor John Polkinghorne, once Professor of Mathematical Physics at the University of Cambridge, is now a priest of the Church of England. He brings out one obvious difference in this way: 'Science is very successful in settling questions; so that during my professional lifetime we have found out about a new level in the structure of matter which we had not known about before. We now all agree that is the case. In religion, we do not have that power to settle issues to universal satisfaction. Debate about the existence of God continues and will continue. I think the difference between the two arises from science's power to manipulate its materials and take a rather impersonal and detached view of what is going on. Religion involves a personal element, which gives the experience it is concerned with a unique quality. Science and religion both search for truth; but science is concerned with the impersonal and general; whereas religion is concerned with the personal and unique; and there you lack that amount of universal agreement.'

It certainly seems very odd to think about experimenting on God. For a start, we could not possibly have the power to do such a thing; and even if we did, it would seem somehow improper, as improper as carrying out experiments on other human beings. We do not experiment on people, when we are trying to love them. So if, as Christians think, the chief aim of human life is to love God, it will hardly be possible for us to think of experimenting on him. We cannot manipulate God. We cannot take a detached, impersonal view of whether he exists or not. And we cannot predict what he is going to do, since he is more like a free person than like a bunch of electrons moving in predictable – or partly predictable – patterns. It is because religious beliefs – or, at any rate, beliefs about God – deal with this personal and unpredictable character of God that the usual forms of scientific investigation and explanation cannot deal with them. That doesn't at all mean they can't exist. It means that there are questions – about our personal relationships, the values we have and the meaning of our lives – which the natural sciences cannot, and do not wish to, explain.

Nevertheless, within its own proper realm, science continues to provide profound and exciting insights into the way the world is. As Professor Polkinghorne says, 'I believe that the regularities science discerns in the world are reflections of the faithfulness of the creator. Religion is able to seek to answer questions that arise out of science itself, deeper questions which are beyond science's power to answer, but which science suggests to us – questions such as, "Why can we understand the world?" Science is essentially concerned with taking given law and circumstance, which it tries to discern in the world, and explaining the things that go on in the world in terms of them. It is very successful at doing that. But the delicate balance and structure of the laws that we find in the world and its beautiful, elegant and economical character, when expressed mathematically, those are things that science just accepts as given. But they are very striking facts about the world; and to many scientists they seem to call for a deeper explanation. Because science assumes them to be so, it can't explain them itself. But if we see these things as reflections of the character of God conveyed to the world he has created, we would find a deeper and more satisfying explanation in that thought.'

This is by no means a new idea. Isaac Newton himself understood his work as unravelling the laws that a perfectly wise and powerful God would have put into the world, if he was going to make it as mathematically elegant and simple as possible. There seems to a scientist to be something deeply unacceptable about the thought that we have to end by saying, 'Well, that is just the way it is; take it or leave it; there is no further explanation.' He may have to stop there; but as John Polkinghorne says, 'Science creates the feeling that there is more to the world than meets the eye. There are things that are striking about the world that science accepts without being able to explain. In that sense, science motivates a search for a deeper understanding of those things. A religious understanding is one possible understanding of the world. It is not an inevitable one; there is no unique and logically coercive way of going from a scientific world-view to a wider world-view. But the two do seem to fit together and complement each other in a way that is coherent, and to me persuasive and intellectually attractive.'

A physicist such as Polkinghorne, then, sees the world as having the character of intellectual beauty; as showing an amazingly delicate balance and order which arouses awe and wonder as we see it. This is not only consistent with the thought of a wise creator; it almost inevitably leads the mind to that hypothesis. Indeed, it might even be said, not that science leads to God, but that it is the idea of God which gives birth to science as we know it. The world as physics sees it is not just 'one damn thing after another'. It is a highly ordered and beautiful structure, and it is natural for anyone with a scientific mind to ask, 'Why is it the way it is?' If we press this question, as Professor Polkinghorne says, we have to go beyond the scope of science itself. And then a natural, though not an inevitable, answer is to say that it is the creation of a personal God who intends it to realise certain values which would not otherwise exist. That is certainly a better explanation than a view which says that it is just there by accident. Yet it may seem to conflict with the way the world looks to the untutored eye of common sense. If we look at our planet, with its innumerable wars and natural catastrophes; if we regard the incidence of wasting disease and crippling disfigurement; if we consider the cruelties of the natural order, in which animals have to kill each other to survive; then the world may seem both senseless and unjust. It is easy to think that if there is any creator of such a world, he must be a sadistic or perhaps an incompetent God – as David Hume once suggested, a baby God, just beginning to learn how to do it. But a knowledge of physics shows us a different picture: a picture of a universe of interlocking energy patterns, balanced in the most intricate and elegant ways; a universe of order and subtlety, the product of a being of enormous wisdom, whom Albert Einstein called 'the Old One'.

How can we square the harsh God of chance with the infinitely wise designer of the intelligible cosmos? I think we have to begin by acknowledging that the universe is a product of enormous rationality and wisdom. It is a universe in which the parts are so interlinked that one part of it could not be changed without causing enormous changes elsewhere in the structure. Its general structure is one of necessity; though, as we have seen, within these necessities there is room for a degree of indeterminacy or chance. We might hazard the thought that this is the universe God had to make, if beings anything like us were to exist at all. He could not have created beings like us – sentient animals, formed of material substance – in a totally different universe. Thus the universe is, in general, necessarily what it is; and it expresses one aspect of the nature of the creator, a nature which he himself cannot change, since it too is necessarily what it is. Its interplay of chance and necessity is what is required to generate the evolution of free rational creatures. In such a universe, the elegant interplay of its fundamental elements will result, at a macrocosmic level, in the appearance of haphazard and uncaring processes, involving much suffering and disaster as well as much happiness and good fortune. As the prophet Isaiah makes God say: 'I form the light and create darkness, I bring prosperity and create disaster' (Isaiah 45,7).

It is useless for the creature to question the creator, as Job discovered. Yet even if we can see how reason gives rise to the appearance of randomness, and how necessity gives rise to the appearance of contingency, could we bring ourselves to call such a creator 'good'? While belief in the wisdom of God lies in the study of nature, belief in the goodness of God lies in moral experience, and so, strictly speaking, it lies beyond the confines of this Chapter. But it would be a naive understanding of the goodness of God which led us to expect that he would do no harm. It would certainly not be a Biblical understanding of the Hebrew God of plagues and battles. In the Biblical context, God's goodness consists in three things: he is himself beyond corruption and evil; he demands of us that we should seek justice and holiness; and, while he ruthlessly punishes injustice, he is patient and forgiving, if we turn to him. That is, he is able to bring all things finally to fulfilment; though he himself, the New Testament suggests, must undergo a baptism of suffering (Mark 10,39) before this can be accomplished.

This is only the outline of an approach to this most difficult of all problems, for the Christian. My suggestion is that we must escape from the picture of a God who does not want to do any harm, and who is able to do absolutely anything he wants at any time. If we have such a picture, the problem of innocent suffering is quite insoluble. But modern science does help us to have a larger concept of God, and one more in line with Christian tradition. We see God then as the necessary basis of the intelligibility of the cosmos, who cannot change its character without destroying it entirely. And in faith we may believe that he is able to bring good out of the evil we must undergo in this universe; so that in the end nothing will be wasted of all that we have done and suffered in the created world. Suffering is generated from the essential being of God himself; he does not just choose to create it, when he has a better alternative. God's goodness lies in his determination to bring all created things to good; and he calls us to share in this process, as we are able. Further than that, we cannot go, without knowing the answer to that final question, 'What explains God?'

If we knew that, we would *be* God; that is, we would be omniscient. But it is a fascinating fact that many physicists now are exploring the idea of discovering an ultimately self-existent and self-explanatory being; one that has to be the way it is and that provides an ultimate rationality, value and purpose simply by the fact of its own existence. 'We want a sense of logical inevitability,' says Steven Weinberg, a leading American nuclear physicist – not just an ultimate unexplained fact, but something that will explain its own existence, if only we could understand it. Some physicists posit that the material universe itself may be such a thing. Dr Peter Atkins, in an elegant little book, *The Creation*, tries to develop a mathematical theory that would make the universe itself totally self-explanatory. If that could be done, there would be no need to introduce God. But I suspect that what is happening is that the universe itself is being made into something more like God than may have been suspected by Newton. For the extraordinary fact is that the traditional Christian definition of God, given by Thomas Aquinas in the thirteenth century and by most of the early fathers of the church, is exactly what these physicists are now talking about and wanting. The traditional Christian God is not a person who just happens, by accident, to be there. The 'Five

Ways' of Thomas Aquinas, in his great work, the *Summa Theologiae*, are often taken as proofs of God. But it can be more helpful to see them as definitions of what sort of thing God is. God turns out to be the one and only self-existent being, the only being which depends on nothing else for its existence, but on which all other things depend. For Aquinas, all finite things in space and time are contingent – they may or may not exist; they do not account for their own existence; they stand in need of explanation in terms of something else. Now the objection to seeing the universe itself as self-existent is that it is, in the end, just a collection of contingent things. And how can a group of things all of which depend on something else account for its own existence?

Christian theologians have always said that, in the end, we can never fully comprehend what God is. But we can say, in outline at least, what sort of being he would be. We can say that he would be the only fully satisfying explanation of the way the world is. Now I am not claiming that all, or even most, physicists, believe in God. The easiest way to be an atheist is just to say that, beautiful and elegant though the universe is, in a mathematical sense, it has no ultimate explanation. We must just accept that it is the way it is. Physics will certainly not prove otherwise. My aim is a more modest one – to show that physics is not in a position of rooted antagonism to religious belief. And, more positively, to show that modern physics is actually very sympathetic to a certain kind of theism, even if it does not compel acceptance of it. The sympathy is this – that physicists are positing, as the ideal completion of their own search for truth and the intellectual beauty of being, something having many characteristics of the traditional Christian idea of God. One could say, as a physicist, that such an ideal is just that – an ideal, without any correspondence to reality. Or one can, like Dr Atkins, try to show that the universe itself is self-explanatory and necessarily what it is. But it seems to me a probable supposition that the necessary and uncaused being which is the cause of all things in the universe is itself other than the universe, and is a rational substance which brings the universe into being as an expression in time of its eternal nature.

This is not, of course, a 'proof' of God. The move to the ultimate explanation is not a coercive one. But it is a very natural one; and we might say that the postulate of such a God is confirmed by the perceived structure of the universe. The roots of belief in God will not themselves lie in science, however. Professor Polkinghorne says, for example, 'The principle source of my Christian faith is my Christian experience – the worship of God; trying to understand and come to terms with the figure of Christ. My scientific view of the world obviously does not impinge very closely upon that. But the two do rub up against each other at the fringes. If it is true that there is purpose and meaning in the world, that will find some reflection within the scientific structure of the world. And so the delicate balance and the beautiful intelligibility of the world are encouraging to faith; but they are not the main source of faith. That lies in more personal experience.' This can hardly be unexpected. It would be a bit odd, after all, if God was just an abstract extrapolation from physics. He is not part of any scientific formula. God must be a personal reality, known first of all in one's own life and in the community of faith. But belief in God cannot be kept in a separate compartment, away from all other knowledge. And, as we have seen, one of the problems about religious belief in our culture is that people think it incompatible with science, or with that vaguer animal, 'the scientific world-view'. What I have tried to bring out here is that such a popularly held view is quite wrong. When properly understood, the scientific world-view both springs from and leads back to the religious world-view. What we need to see is the pretty obvious truth that not all questions are scientific questions. And, of course, sometimes new discoveries in science will mean that we have to readjust our understanding of things, and give up views, such as the belief that the universe was created six thousand years ago, which clearly contradict a vast body of scientific knowledge. We will go on having intellectual problems; but that is just what we should expect, if we think that we have not yet got the total truth about everything. There is no basic conflict at all between religion and science, as such.

Professor Polkinghorne agrees with Paul Davies that there have been vast changes in the sciences in recent years. 'We have come to realise in this century that when we probe the structure of matter to its very roots, the clear and determinate and reliable world of everday dissolves away. The quantum world that we have discovered in this century is cloudy and fitful. We cannot picture what is going on in it and it is not absolutely open to our prediction. We can only speak of the probabilities of what might happen. The world is much stranger and much looser in its structure than Newton or the great physicists of the nineteenth century could ever have imagined. So we cannot say with certainty what is going to happen. We can only say: this is likely, or that is less likely. And on a particular occasion, one or the other might happen. Moreover we cannot actually assign a cause why one or other actually happens on a given occasion. So we have lost that totally predictable universe.'

This echoes what Professor Bartholomew was saying – that chance now plays a major part in our understanding of the universe. It does not mean there is no order or plan. But it does mean that the universe is much more open to new initiatives and impulses, much less predetermined; it is more creative, a freer universe than Newton had thought. It is, perhaps, not so much a machine as a growing, creative, almost organic system, in which each part reflects every other to produce as yet unrealised states of being. Such a universe allows scope for the providential action of God, just as it allows for the acts and purposes of human beings. We should not think of these acts, human or divine, as jumping into the gaps left in the structure by indeterminacy. That would be a most unfortunate image. It is rather that, since we live in what Polkinghorne calls a 'cloudier' universe, not everything about that universe can be exhaustively captured by a set of mechanistic laws, as if you were dealing with a closed system which allowed no other sorts of explanation to exist. John Polkinghorne says: 'The universe is more open than the very closed and tightly restricted world that Newton thought about. If we are to look for things like meaning and purpose in the world – which I certainly think we find there, and which are of course essential to a religious understanding of the world – it will not be through the ricketiness of things, through little gaps. It will be through looking at the world from a totally different perspective, a perspective that is consistent with the reliability that science sees, but which functions at a different level of interpretation.'

The idea is that, just as we would not call free human acts interventions in nature, or contradictions of physical laws, so we need not call God's actions interventions in nature or contradictions of nature's laws. Human acts can be purposive, and not included in any set of scientific statements about the movements of particles. Once we get away from the old machine-analogy, we can see that laws are general mathematical functions which we use to express certain regularities of interaction between material particles, other things being equal. But those laws do not by any means describe the whole of the phenomena of nature. Modern physics forces us to see that the laws do not give a complete and wholly determined picture of the universe. They pick out certain patterns which we can express mathematically and probabilistically. They do tell us what the universe is like; but many other perspectives or ways of looking at the world are possible, too; and they would be needed in any full account of what there is. On the old view, the universe was a totally predictable machine, which God had to tinker with if he was going to do anything. Modern physics sees the universe as a developing, interactive organic unity, which can be described from many perspectives, in many ways. What is 'cloudy' or 'rickety' from one point of view simply shows the limitations of our own descriptive schemes; and it may be wholly natural from another point of view, when we speak of meaning and purpose, and of forms of personal interaction between creatures and between God and creation as a whole.

I shall be touching on the subject of miracles in Chapter Five, but it should now be apparant that modern physics has little reason to rule them out as impossible. Miracles may seem very unnatural from one point of view – the point of view which only considers general and regular laws in their normal conditions of operation. But they may be entirely natural from another, wider, point of view, from which they play a part in disclosing the meaning and purpose of the creation as a whole, as events in which fairly unique sets of conditions obtain, because of historical circumstances and so on. We may need many complementary ways of speaking to give us an adequate view of how the world really is. And there is no reason why the language of religion should not provide one such perspective which is able to communicate to us precisely that meaning and purpose of which the sciences see expressions and hints, but which lie beyond their scope to embrace.

There are a number of ways, then, in which contemporary physics has transformed our view of the universe, and made it much more conducive to a religious understanding. We are not faced with a blunt opposition between a valueless, purposeless world of brute facts and a set of purely personal preferences, inhabiting some hidden recesses in our skulls. Modern physics brings to our attention a world which forces on us the ultimate questions, 'Why is there anything?' 'Why are the basic laws as they are?' and 'What is the nature of the world?' It shows that these are not silly and pointless questions; but the very stuff of physics itself; that it is more rational to seek an answer than to shrug one's shoulders and give up. Physics reveals the elegance and beauty of the universe; it shows the existence of an intelligibility in things which seems to express a wisdom far greater than our own, but supremely rational. Then physics reminds us that the ultimate constituents of matter are quite unpicturable; they dissolve into probability-waves and complex energy-patterns, in which the distinction of whole and part is strangely interwoven, and in which it is the action of the observer which resolves probabilities into actualities.

This strange, cloudy and fitful world dispenses with the materialism of the clockwork universe, and invites us to contemplate a world open to sorts of influence and action we can scarcely conceive, but which may be the vehicle of meaning and even be inwardly orientated towards our own existence, instead of being intolerably alien and unconcerned. Physics, too, points out the extraordinary amount of fine structure and tuning in the universe, and thus strongly suggests an underlying purpose in its processes. And finally, it makes clear the partial nature of all our interpretative schemes of explanation, and thus leaves open the possibility of higher sorts of interpretation, not reducible to lower levels, which disclose uniqueness, meaning and purpose in things. There may be no proofs of God in physics. But it is no longer true that physics has rendered God superfluous. On the contrary, it is the strongest indicator that our physical world is founded on universal principles so elegant and beautiful, so ordered and interrelated, that it suggests to the mind with almost overwhelming force that the basis of this world is one rational and conscious creator, who has imprinted in the heavens and on the earth the manifest marks of his handiwork.

Chapter Three
FAITH AND REASON

In 1936 the philosopher A. J. Ayer wrote a delightful and incisive book, *Language, Truth and Logic*, in which he managed to dispense with the existence of God in eight short pages. He was making available to the English public a school of philosophical thought deriving from the Vienna Circle, widely known as Logical Positivism. The Positivists used one simple principle, the Verification Principle, which said that a statement has a meaning if and only if there is some way of verifying it – of showing it to be true by appeal to some possible sense-experience. Now the existence of God cannot be shown to be true by appeal to any sense-experiences; nobody can ever see, touch or feel God. So God is meaningless; the word is just gobbledegook. The whole of theology can be thrown out of the window as so much verbiage, without sense. So Ayer could say that he wasn't even an atheist – somebody who denies the existence of God. He couldn't deny that God existed, because he didn't even know what the word 'God' meant.

The whole question of God seemed to some to be so peripheral that it was not even of interest to philosophers any more. When Bryan Magee made a series for TV called *Men of Ideas*, he managed to make sixteen programmes about modern philosophy without mentioning religion once. I remember that when I asked him once why this was, he said there was no such subject as philosophy of religion.

Now this seems a bit odd in a way, because I am supposed to be the Professor of the Philosophy of Religion in the University of London. But perhaps, like God, I shouldn't exist. However, it is true that British philosophy did pass through a phase of almost total lack of interest in God and religion. It was a phase of rather short duration. At the beginning of this century, philosophers like F. H. Bradley, who was the dominant figure in British philosophy for a good many years, J. M. McTaggart and Bernard Bosanquet were busily talking about God and the Absolute for much of the time. But then something peculiar seemed to happen. Bertrand Russell, G. E. Moore and A. J.

Ayer appeared on the scene, and the old style of philosophy ceased to exist overnight. Instead, a new, incisive, precise, no-nonsense philosophy took over and dominated English universities, at least.

Sir Alfred Ayer is now probably the best-known philosopher in Britain. In fact, it is possible that he is the only living philosopher most people have ever heard of. Even though he remains staunchly opposed to Christianity and has been President of the British Humanist Association, it would be almost impossible to try to give a view of modern British philosophy of religion without taking account of his views. Those views, of course, have changed quite a lot in the course of the fifty years since *Language, Truth and Logic* was first published. Sir Alfred says, 'I think that a lot of it is wrong; I would not write it in the same way if I were writing it today. It is not surprising if my thought has moved a little; it would be rather shocking if it had not.' A more recent statement of his thought can be found in *The Central Questions of Philosophy*, where it becomes apparent that God cannot be dispensed with in quite so short a way. Ayer was indeed rather surprised that his views at the time proved so influential, causing flutters in pulpits up and down the land with such a little expenditure of energy.

'At that time I held what was called the Principle of Verification; that for a proposition to be significant it had to be empirically testable or else formally true. I argued that propositions about an other-worldly being such as the Christian God was supposed to be were literally nonsensical. I just stated this dogmatically and an extraordinary number of people seemed to be convinced by my assertion. In a later treatment of the subject, I was not quite so radical. It is possible that the existence of God is an explanatory hypothesis; but I would still dismiss it on the grounds that it explains nothing.' Ayer has by no means come round to believing in God; but he is much more sympathetic to the concept, as a philosophically possible and even interesting one. When he could say that the whole idea of God was nonsense, there was no point in trying to talk about it. But if it is an explanatory hypothesis, then we may at least have to take it seriously, and ask whether and how it explains anything. The demise of the Verification Principle has thus opened up the question of God for philosophers again in a new way.

It is important to see that the Verification Principle no longer has any force as a criterion of meaning, that is, as a way of ruling out some assertions as pure nonsense. But it may be held in a very weak form, as a sort of request that any assertion must make some sort of difference to experience that can be tested. But now, the principle begins to look very vague and even rather waffly. As Ayer says, 'I am not sure in what form I want to hold the principle. In *Language, Truth and Logic*, it was rather ambiguous. I did not there make a distinction between what was verifiable by the speaker, being the person that he was, and what was verifiable by some sort of ideal observer. I never solved that question; I never decided which form of the principle I was using, and that to a very large extent vitiates the book. My present tendency would be to take the more impersonal, ideal observer view. But the notion of an "ideal observer" is a very obscure one, and perhaps it is not clear enough to make good sense.' So, by one of those beautiful ironic twists that adorn the history of philosophy, it turns out that the principle which was to be used to show religious assertions to be unintelligible may itself be unintelligible. The idea of an 'ideal observer', who could verify things in the distant past or in distant parts of space or in the minds of other people and animals, is just about as obscure as the idea of God – to which, if the truth be told, it bears an uncanny resemblance.

The ideal observer comes in, because if you say that you must be able to test the truth of any factual assertion by having some sense-experience, you are at once in difficulty about the past. How can any sense-experience of yours now show that something really happened in the past? So you invent an ideal observer, who can travel back in time, and observe it. But what if I say that last night I dreamed of a zebra? That is a factual assertion; but can even an ideal observer test it? Only if he can enter my dreams, while I am asleep. That is the sort of knowledge only a being rather like God could have. And it really looks as if we must just admit that some factual claims cannot be tested, even in principle. A simple and persuasive case is the claim that lobsters feel pain when they are boiled alive. There is no way of testing this without being a lobster; and if you were a lobster, you could not communicate your feelings; so there is a straightforward, and very important, factual claim which is untestable. Does it make any difference? Well, it makes a difference to the lobster; but it does not affect any predictions I may make, or any observations I may have. In that sense, it explains nothing: but it is still a factual statement.

'By the early seventies,' Ayer says, 'I had ceased to use the Verification Principle as a hatchet, in the way that I used to. But I was still requiring that any proposition should in some way be testable. I still held it in a very weak form. And by that time I was allowing the possibility that religious propositions might have a function, if they were genuinely explanatory in the way a scientific proposition was. I argued that they were not; that they failed this test, because they were consistent with anything that happened.' I have just mentioned a case where a factual assertion does seem to be consistent with anything that happens, so far as we can observe it; so I cannot agree with Professor Ayer here. But it should be noted how very weak this principle of verification now is. It really allows in virtually anything. For example, our lobster can be admitted, because we can say that its writhings and twitchings, and facts about its nervous system, or lack of it, are *relevant* to its feelings of pain. True, we cannot observe the pain itself. But we can observe behaviour and the structure of the nervous system; and these things give us some grounds for ascribing pain to lobsters. We cannot be certain. For us, though not perhaps for the poor lobster, it is a hypothesis that it feels pain. But some observable facts are relevant to its feeling pain; in that sense, it is very weakly verifiable. But now, in that sense, God is weakly verifiable, too. For there are certainly lots of human experiences which are relevant to the existence of God, which suggest it as a likely hypothesis. These are precisely such facts as the order and apparent design in nature, experiences of the presence of a personal reality, and events such as fulfilments of prophecy and miracles. Of course people will argue about such things; they are by no means beyond dispute. Other explanations may well suggest themselves; and they will have to be evaluated, too. But it is just not true that theism is consistent with anything; it does lead us to expect certain sorts of experiences rather than others; and so it comes within the ambit of the weak verification principle after all.

It is a most relevant point that Professor Ayer himself has never had any religious experiences. Interestingly enough, though, he seems to know what a religious experience might be; otherwise, how would he know he had never had one? And if he knows what a religious experience might be, then he knows something which would tend to confirm belief in God, if it occurred. 'I have never had what I would call a religious experience. I was baptised into the Church of England, but neither of my parents were church-goers. At the age of about fifteen, I suddenly thought to myself, "Do I believe all this?", and decided that I did not; and since then I have never looked back.' It is perhaps because of this apparently total lack of religious experience that Ayer can say, 'One reason for not believing Christianity is that there is not the slightest evidence in its favour. So I do not believe it any more than I believe there is a rhinoceros in the room.' But of course from a theist's point of view, to compare God to a rhinoceros in the living-room is a travesty of belief. And this comment shows very clearly why it is very difficult for an empiricist – a philosopher who tries to derive all knowledge from sense-experience – to believe in God. Since God is supposed not to be a physical object or a sensation, there is no way for the empiricist to get to know God at all. But that may mean that there is something wrong with empiricism, not that there is something wrong with God. And indeed, empiricism itself seems to have collapsed in recent years.

Sometimes people do not realise what an odd theory empiricism really is. In its classical British form, as developed by Locke, Berkeley and Hume, in the seventeenth and eighteenth centuries, and as represented so elegantly and clearly by Ayer in this century, it holds that all knowledge must derive from, or be based on, sensory experiences, often called sense-data. But this is not a common-sense view at all. Common sense assumes that we have knowledge that physical objects continue to exist unobserved; that some physical entities, like electrons, can exist even though we can never observe them directly; that other minds exist, with thoughts and feelings which the rest of us can never get into; and that the past really existed, even though we can never get back to it. Common sense, in other words, takes a realist view of the world – that we know a real world of physical objects. We come to know it by means of our sensory experiences, of course. But we do not have to infer its existence from sense-data; we know it directly. And we know many things about it that we can never directly check by sense-experience – for example, that things exist when we are not looking at them. We all assume they do; but every time we try to check it, we have to look at them, and so we never catch them unobserved. How, then, do we know it? A realist will say that this is just basic knowledge. We do not infer it from anything else, not even from sense-experiences. It is basic to all our beliefs, a sort of fundamental assumption without which we cannot have knowledge of the world at all.

Now once you allow such fundamental assumptions, the believer in God can say that belief in God is a basic belief, too. It does not have to be inferred from anything else; it is rather a fundamental assumption, that we do not only have knowledge of a world of physical objects, but we also have knowledge of a unique reality conceived by analogy with a conscious self or will, which is both directly knowable and often mediated through or manifested in the world of finite things. God is not either like an object in the world – an invisible rhinoceros – or like an explanatory hypothesis, or purely theoretical entity. He is a directly knowable reality; but to know him requires a certain commitment, a renunciation of selfish desire and an adoption of the practice of prayer and contemplation. For a realist, this is certainly a respectable position to take. But empiricists like Professor Ayer insist that the common-sense view cannot just be taken as basic.

'In two or three of my later books I have tried to show how the common-sense view can be developed as a theory on a sensory basis. I try to show how the structure of our sensory experience is such that it justifies the positing of common-sense physical objects.' It turns out, then, that the world of physical objects is itself an explanatory hypothesis, for Ayer. In this respect, it is rather like what he takes belief in God to be, except, of course, that belief in a God would be a much higher level theory. There is a hierarchy of theories. First, the fundamental level of sensation; then the common-sense theory; then the various physical theories, that bear much the same relation to common sense as common sense bears to the original sensory data; then more abstract physical theories and so on. The hypothesis of God would be on the most general level of all. But, as we have seen, Ayer's objection to it is that it helps us to predict nothing; it is empty. However, if belief in physical objects is an explanatory theory, it is also empty; it is consistent with whatever happens. Indeed, if it is not, it is no good as a theory. What would falsify the belief that there are physical objects? I suppose, in theory, that if we one day awoke to find that we were disembodied spirits who had been having a particularly bad dream, that would do it. But this is a fantastic example; and we know very well that nothing like that is going to happen. The hypothesis that physical objects exist is not explanatory in the way a scientific theory is – it does not predict exactly what will happen, or provide general mathematical laws. It makes no difference at all to our experience – except, perhaps, that it is useful to help to simplify and make sense of our experiences.

So, if we take the hypothesis of God, it could be falsified, in principle. We could wake up to find the universe was controlled by three malignant demons, who loved torturing human beings. Of course, this example is fantastic, too. In practice, we do not expect to falsify the existence of God. Yet certain experiences threaten to do so – the existence of great suffering, for instance. Other experiences help to confirm it – experiences of being guided, comforted, challenged or empowered by a beneficent power – the sort of experiences Alister Hardy finds so common, though they are not shared by Alfred Ayer. So the hypothesis of God is no more empty than the hypothesis of a world of physical objects; and, though it is very general, it is not consistent with absolutely anything that might happen.

We might say that the postulate of God is not a scientific hypothesis, but a metaphysical one. But, someone might say, is metaphysics not dead, in the twentieth century? The answer is, quite certainly not; it is alive and flourishing. As Ayer says, 'British philosophy has emerged from the positivism that I to some extent initiated. It has taken a different direction; an interest in language is a dominant theme, and there is more convergence between science and philosophy now than there was. I myself do allow a role to metaphysics, as proposing an alternative conceptual system; but I argue that, to be acceptable, it has to bear an intelligible relation to our actual conceptual system. But there might be revisions to our actual system that would count as metaphysical, and would be acceptable. Indeed, studying the most general features of our language could itself be called a sort of metaphysics.'

Metaphysics, then, can be seen as the study of the most general features of a conceptual system; and it is all right to tidy up our actual system a bit to get a more elegant or coherent one. Since the idea of God is central to conceptual systems of many people, it turns out that the construction of metaphysical systems centring on the idea of God is a possible and proper philosophical activity.

To many of us, that is no surprise, since that is what a great number of the best known classical philosophers have always done – people like Descartes, Leibniz, Spinoza, Kant and Hegel. But perhaps to find Sir Alfred Ayer, the scourge of the metaphysicians and believers in the thirties, saying it now, fifty years later, illustrates a change in climate that has come over British philosophy in this century. It is not that all philosophers have turned into believers. Ayer is just as anti-Christian as he ever was. But religious belief can no longer be easily dismissed as nonsense or illusion; and philosophical arguments against it are now seen to be highly disputable and often not very compelling.

Richard Swinburne is Professor of the Philosophy of the Christian Religion at Oxford. He has written three major books arguing for the rationality of belief in God, as well as more technical works in philosophy on confirmation theory and space and time. He sums up the change of mood in the following way: 'In the 1950s there was a tradition of philosophy in Oxford called "ordinary language philosophy", in which the task of philosophy was seen to be simply analysing ordinary usage. Bu that era, I am glad to say, is past, and the temporary lapse of philosophy into the mere study of ordinary language has been superseded. It started to go about 1960, when P. F. Strawson made the word "metaphysics" fashionable again. I think one can say that since then in the Anglo-American philosophical tradition the majority of philosophers have seen themselves as doing metaphysics, that is, giving a very general picture of what the world is like, what things there are in it and what we can know about it. The age-old philosophical problems that philosophers have been talking about for two thousand years are central to metaphysics – mind and body, free will, materialism and so on. And they are still central subjects of discussion.'

In view of this, it may seem odd that some people still seem to think that Positivism, of A. J. Ayer's sort, has killed off metaphysics for ever. But, as Swinburne says, 'There are many sorts of Positivism; but the most ordinary sort is itself a strong metaphysical position – that the only things in the world are things that we can have knowledge of. I think that is a mistaken metaphysical position, but not greatly so; and it is an interesting one. It was ordinary language philososphy which opposed metaphysics; and that was a temporary aberration. The difficulty is that what is taught in philosophical circles is absorbed by the students of one generation; they become the schoolteachers and radio producers of the next generation; and impart to a further generation the orthodoxy of their grand-parents. But in the meanwhile things are moving on.'

At the present time we are faced with a number of competing metaphysical systems; and the two major ones are perhaps materialism – the doctrine that nothing exists except material objects in space – and theism. Many present-day philosophers defend materialism – Anthony Quinton, J. J. C. Smart and J. L. Mackie are perhaps the best known, among philosophers at least. It is a bold and provocative view which, in its modern form, comes from an influential school of philosophy in Sydney, Australia. Swinburne is perhaps the major exponent of theism, 'the doctrine, common to Judaism, Christianity and Islam, that there is a God who sustains the world in being, who keeps the laws of nature operative and who brings about the existence of conscious beings, who themselves have an opportunity to mould the world.'

Swinburne has developed, in a very rigorous and technical way, a number of arguments for the existence of God. 'Just as the physicist does not observe his gluons, his muons and his quarks, but infers them in order to provide the best explanation of the things he can observe; so I think equally good arguments can be given for the existence of God. We know that there is a very orderly universe – everything in infinite time and space obeys exactly the same laws, conforming with perfect regular-ity, wherever it is in time or space. That is such a remarkable coincidence that I think any philososphy which fails to make it a central building-point of its system has got something very badly wrong with it. And we note other facts about the universe – there are conscious beings, capable of responsible action; religion and religious experience is a pervasive phenomenon – many people claim that they are aware of the presence of God; and they should be believed, unless there is some good argument against it. So, starting from phenomena like these, the religious philosopher asks, how best can we account for these facts? The answer is, you account for them in the simplest way you can, by supposing one being controlling the evolution of the universe, and bringing it into being.'

I do not myself suppose that Christians believe in God as a result of some complicated inference; and I do not think Swinburne is suggesting they do. You may well believe in God because of certain experiences of your own. But if you think there is a God who created the universe, then of course you must sooner or later ask if the universe is such that a good and omnipotent God could have made it; or if it seems to point to God as the best explanation of its nature. It is here that metaphysical arguments come in. A good hypothesis should be a simple one, which leads you to expect the data you observe. The method is very much the same as that in science, except that the sciences start off from rather small regions, whereas religion starts off from the vast things already observed which need explaining. We already have the evidence before us; and it is up to us to make sense of it. In Swinburne's view, these arguments will lead us to the conclusion that probably, though not certainly, there is a God.

Swinburne's robust metaphysical claims raise lots of arguments among philosophers, but no one, to my knowledge, says that they are silly or out-dated or unworthy of consideration. On the contrary, they have made the whole issue of arguments for the existence of God a live one again, among professional philosophers. Theism, we might say, has gone onto the attack; and we can see very clearly how it joins hands with science in proposing the possibility of making God the best explanation of how the world actually is.

It is obvious that Professor Swinburne does not think much of ordinary language philosophy. And it has probably become extinct in Britain, in its original form. But it is still true that one of the chief influences on modern British philosophy was Ludwig Wittgenstein, who was chiefly interested, if not in ordinary language, at least in the forms and structure of language. Wittgenstein is a man whom it is very hard to discuss without terrible over-simplification. But while he could hardly be described as a conventional Christian, he insisted on describing himself as a Roman Catholic throughout his life, and at one time said that he would regard it as a sort of self-betrayal to have renounced this allegiance into which he was born. He wrote very little on religion, but the influence of his work has been enormous. Many of the people he taught have become Christians, and he dealt with religious and philosophical questions with a seriousness which does not at all suggest they are pseudo-problems. Many philosophers now teaching in Britain have developed the general approach which Wittgenstein adopted to these problems, though of course they have added their own distinctive insights, too.

One of the best known of these is Dewi Phillips, Professor of Philosophy in the University of Swansea. He rejects both the insistence of A. J. Ayer that all statements must meet some common test of meaning, and the forthright inductive arguments for God that Swinburne propounds. 'If someone is asked whether religious belief is rationally justifiable, the questioner will probably already have a conception of what is rational prior to asking the question, as if that were perfectly clear. He will wish to bring to the bar of reason, so defined, various human activities and modes of discourse; and they, as it were, have to pass the test of that conception of rationality. My own belief is that there is no one over-reaching universal conception of rationality. Therefore what we need is first of all to try to get to the root of what you mean by rational. It may be that the distinction between the rational and the irrational varies systematically with the human activity that you are talking about.'

The objection to both Ayer and Swinburne, from this point of view, is that they try to make everything meet one common test of reason. Whereas different modes of discourse may each have to be judged on their own terms. We should not try to assimilate religious discourse to scientific or metaphysical discourse; that is itself a philosophical mistake, for Phillips. Philosophers are concerned to discover the meaning of religious discourse, but that must be accepted on its own terms: 'What it is reasonable or unreasonable to do, as the next move in a scientific experiment, depends on the nature of that experiment and what you are trying to do in it. What it is reasonable to do when you back horses and you have so much money left; what it is reasonable to do in a row with your wife; what it is reasonable to say in relation to God – only a madman would say that all these come to the same thing. Yet some philosophers, by keeping language at that level of generality, never get down to the hard task of looking at what religion actually means, in order to see what the distinction of reasonable and unreasonable could come to in religion. Of course, people have asked from outside religion, is it reasonable for me to believe? Instead of taking a blanket answer, one would have to enter the discussion with them, and ask what difficulties they have. Some philosophers have said incredible things, such as "I've never seen God"; but neither have religious believers; so that cannot be essential for belief anyway, and it is a curious reason for not believing.' Philosophers like Ayer, Phillips would claim, misunderstand what religious belief actually is. They have no sympathy with it; that is fair enough; but they should not try to apply inappropriate tests to it.

Religion is about worship and prayer; it is not some kind of scientific experiment. Nor, says Phillips, is it a sort of hopeful waiting for some reasons or verification which will be given later, probably after death. 'After all, according to Christianity, one has been given a full and complete revelation of God in Christ. So if you want to speak of reasons here, the reason for the Christian believing is that he sees God in Christ – that would be the religious reason. If you say to me, we want a reason which is beyond that religious reason, which is a quasi-scientific reason, I would find that almost completely unintelligible.'

Phillips is not impressed by the sorts of arguments Swinburne and some physicists give for God; or perhaps it is just not the sort of God he finds of religious interest. For him, God cannot be properly conceived as a sort of good person, designing the world for the best; so he is very antipathetic to views like those of Swinburne. 'These are not analyses of the religion I am involved in; but perhaps religion does not mean the same to all people. Perhaps they are analyses of certain kinds of religion that people have. Then all we can say is that some are shabbier than others.' The point here, I think, is that religious language must be considered on its own terms. It forms, in Wittgenstein's phrase, a specific language-game, embodied in a specific form of life. We must not confuse it with metaphysical games or explanatory attempts to understand the universe. It has its own distinctive set of meanings, its own sorts of reasons, internal to the practice itself. Phillips again: 'Wittgenstein has exploded certain universalist conceptions of reasonableness. He urges us to look at actual usages of language, instead of imposing on one language-use a paradigm from some other branch of language and assuming it must conform to it.'

The task facing the philosopher, on this view, is to understand what is going on in language. He must pay attention to the concepts at work and not impose alien concepts upon the language he is concerned with. So if one asks if religious language, for example, is reasonable, one should not be concerned with some kind of imperial reason, imposing a pseudo-sovereign conception of reason on everything from the outside. One should rather look very carefully at the phenomena themselves to see what kind of phenomena they are. One of the great influences Wittgenstein has had is in showing the great variety there is in human language, the variety in meaning. Logic is not, as the Positivists thought, some kind of *a priori* standard determining what sense and nonsense is prior to all human discourse. It is only within human discourse that the distinction between sense and nonsense is grasped. Since human discourse is various, what that distinction comes to is not given once and for all.

Much philosophy is far too general and does not get down to the detailed analysis of religious language, how we use it, on what occasions and for what purposes and so on. Philosophers after Wittgenstein know that they must pay attention to what is there, instead of making philosophical stipulations about what must be there, before they look. As an example, Professor Phillips takes the question, is religious language literal or metaphorical? 'By literal, people often mean factual; but I would deny that the statement "there is a God" is a statement of fact – as if we could find out, investigate, as if we could be wrong, as if we have modes of enquiry to determine whether it is the case and so on. That does not mean it is not literal; it is literal, since it is used in the primary way which is appropriate to the context in which you are speaking. My view is that religious believers mean what they say literally, without that either being metaphorical or factual. The meaning of the statement "God exists" does not come from philosophy or physics, but from the religious context in which that meaning has its life and force.'

If we oversimplify this view a little, it can be put in a famous aphorism of Wittgenstein's, 'Meaning is use.' The meaning of religious assertions lies, not in something very obscure that they refer to, but in the way they are actually used, in human life. Phillips is surely right to say that beliefs about God are not held, by religious believers, as tentative explanatory hypotheses, or parts of grand metaphysical theories about the nature of everything. 'Faith is putting your trust in something you think it worth putting your trust in; not because you hope it will turn out to be the case in the future, but because you appreciate its spiritual worth now. Faith is communion with the spirit of God now; that is what coming to know God means. What is incredible is talk of God as an object whereas "God" is what you mean by what is of worth. That is why you worship it. It is not a wait and see; it is proving now, in communion with God, the value of your commitment. It is a matter of giving yourself to, or being possessed by, the spirit of God.'

Faith, according to Phillips, is a total commitment to what you take to be of supreme worth. It is quite different from an experimental hypothesis. And it does not involve the theoretical assertion that some object – 'God' – of a rather peculiar sort exists. When we say, for instance, 'God is love', this does not predicate a property of God, which he might not have had. It is saying that one of the meanings of the word God is love. This gives you a rule for the use of the word God. We also say, God is merciful, God is kind, angry and so on; and these are to be understood in terms of what happens when the believer's relationship to that love changes. You might say, 'If you sin against God, he is angry', his love is withdrawn. In fact, you have withdrawn yourself from that love. It is not that you do something and then God decides to hit you over the head. When you say, 'Don't be angry with me', that should be understood in terms of, 'Don't let me become that', rather than 'Don't do that to me'. Believing in the love of God is believing that love, in the form in which it is spelled out in the person of Jesus, for example, can never be defeated.

This can sound very radical, as though Phillips is denying that a real objective God exists. But, while in my view it is phrased in a paradoxical way, it is surprisingly traditional. For the orthodox Christian tradition, God is not an object – Aquinas said that God is not a substance or a member of any class; that is, he is not one example, a very superior one, of a certain kind of thing. And it is true that religious belief is not really an experimental or inductive matter; it is more like a total commitment to a discernment of worth or value. So Phillips belongs to a group of philosophers who are concerned to stress the distinctiveness of religion as a form of human life, with its own proper internal standards of rationality, which primarily governs the way a person lives and the nature of that person's basic commitments and loyalties. The later work of Wittgenstein has helped to establish such a view, in opposition to the simple dismissals of the earlier Positivists. Nevertheless, many philosophers would feel that, while Phillips may be right in his central claims, he still divorces the question of God too much from other areas of human life. Religion does not just exist on its own, after all; and it needs to be related more widely to our other beliefs, about ethics, art and science. While metaphysics may not be the core of living religious belief, in the end such belief has to fit into some overall metaphysical scheme, some picture of the way things really are. Such a task may be so difficult that it may not yet be possible to achieve it; but it is a proper and necessary task, all the same.

'The rejection of metaphysics was one of the primary planks of the Logical Positivist programme. But traditional metaphysical questions are certainly now recognised as entirely legitimate philosophical questions. That particular idea, that metaphysics was to be torn out of philosophy, has been completely abandoned. Whether the traditional partition of philosophy into metaphysics, theory of knowledge, moral philosophy and so on is a good one, I rather doubt. But that is not to repudiate those questions; it is just a matter of classification.' This is the statement of Professor Michael Dummett, Wykeham Professor of Logic at Oxford, and Sir Alfred Ayer's successor. As a Roman Catholic, he takes a very different view of religion from his predecessor. Indeed, it would be to some people an astonishing fact that at the time I write this both the Professors of Philosophy at Cambridge are Catholics and two out of the four Professors of Philosophy at Oxford are Christians of a Catholic tradition. The idea that religious belief is somehow impossible for a philosopher has been well and truly squashed. Dummett says bluntly, 'Logical Positivism has for many years been dead. Even from the early 1960s, it was pretty well completely dead. The ordinary language school faded away a little time after that. But philosophy in Oxford, as in the United States, remains in the analytical tradition, which comes down from Frege, Russell, Moore and Wittgenstein.' Nevertheless, as we have noted, philosophers in this tradition have a new confidence in writing on metaphysical themes. Another eminent Oxford philosopher, Lord Quinton, is the author of a book entitled *The Nature of Things*; J. L. Mackie has written *The Miracle of Theism*; Peter Geach has written *God and the Soul*; and Anthony Kenny, Master of Balliol College and formerly a Catholic priest, has written *Faith and Reason*.

These are not by any means all books defending the idea of

God. On the contrary, some of the most able contain sustained attacks on the coherence of the idea. But they show that metaphysical issues such as this one are being taken with full seriousness. Attacks such as that by J.L. Mackie show a sense of the importance of the issues which contrasts sharply with the dismissiveness of some earlier writers. And defences like those of P.T. Geach display a logical rigour and tightness of argument which makes it quite clear that theism has immense intellectual weight on its side. There is no lack of serious debate about God. But Michael Dummett would accept that, in the earlier years of the analytical movement, not a lot of constructive work was done in this area.

'On the whole this part of philosophy has been very much neglected. I think there is a reason for that. There are certain topics which cannot be fruitfully enquired into until others have been investigated. Philosophy of religion or natural theology has always been rather high in the hierarchy of philosophical topics. If you look, for example, at Thomas Aquinas' writings on God, you cannot properly understand them until you have understood a lot of his more philosophical notions. You cannot properly evaluate them. Now when the revolution in philosophy this century first occurred, it was largely a destructive period. Logical Positivism and, to a considerable extent, the ordinary language school, intended to pull down a great deal that had previously been done in philosophy. What they succeeded in doing consisted chiefly in calling in question various traditional ideas. What has been happening in the last twenty years is the onset of a much more constructive phase. But it is very difficult to get at questions which lie high in the hierarchy of topics, if you are attempting any kind of constructive theorising, until you have done more work lower down.' It is because we are still in the early stages of constructive theorising that not a great deal has been said, in a very positive way, about God. But to see that something is a problem, or that it has not yet been solved, is not to discount it as a vitally important issue. In fact, one of the important lessons the progress of philosophy in this century can teach is that the easy answers may well be much less easy than they seem at first; and that philosophical wisdom consists largely in learning to live with unfathomable problems and to stop looking for simple solutions. There is all the difference in the world between the words of the young Wittgenstein – 'I believe myself to have found, on all essential points, the final solution of the problems' (Preface to the *Tractatus Logico-Philosophicus*), and the subtle, even agonised, explorations of the older Wittgenstein of the *Philosophical Investigations*. Thinking about God is hard; and any easy solutions are likely to be wrong. To get clear about the meaning of 'God', you first have to get clear about meaning; and even that is a subject of hot debate.

Professor Dummett comments: 'The ideas that the Positivists had about meaning have been seen to be pretty thoroughly confused. It is not so much the idea of verification that is wrong, as their conception of what verification consists in. Language is in fact a kind of network. At one end of the spectrum, as it were, there are sentences which can be used as reports of observations. Even those are not, as the Positivists thought, just records of sense-experiences, but what counts as verifying them could be said to be some series of sense-experiences. At the far end of the spectrum there are things like mathematical statements, the verification of which consists solely in a piece of reasoning. Most statements lie somewhere in between. We accept them partly on a basis of observation and partly by some argument based on that observation. This whole thing constitutes the verification of the statement. Once you think in those terms, you no longer have a test for meaning – as if you could say, "Well, this is ruled out because you cannot think of any series of sense-experiences which would confirm it." There are just very, very few sentences in the language whose meaning is given in that simple direct way. That is why I think philosophers have now a much more tolerant attitude to religious statements.' Most philosophers nowadays would reject verification with much more assurance than Dummett would. He wishes to retain a broadened notion; but those who reject the idea of verification completely, and think that the meaning of a statement consists in a grasp of what has to be the case for it to be true, have stronger reason than he has for rejecting the exclusivist views of the Positivists.

So to understand the idea of God you have to understand the sorts of arguments that actually apply in that area, and how they connect – perhaps very indirectly – with observation-statements. There must, in other words, be some arguments in favour of God; and they must ultimately be rooted in experience. Professor Dummett believes that such arguments can be found, and thus that belief in God is wholly rational. 'I do not myself think,' he says, 'that the arguments as formulated in scholastic philosophy, for example by Aquinas, will stand up as formulated; partly because they involve certain philosophical notions that I should not accept. But I do think that there cannot be any reasonable belief in the existence of God unless something which looks roughly like that can be produced. I cannot pretend, however, that I have succeeded in thinking my way through these questions at all to my own satisfaction, let alone anybody else's.'

Professor Dummett does not regard religious faith as just a matter of having good intellectual arguments; it is also, and perhaps primarily, a matter of how one lives, and the part a belief might play in structuring one's life, of the effects of adopting one belief or another. Yet he clearly thinks that there are good intellectual reasons for believing in God. They are, however, so difficult to formulate, and presuppose so much hard logical work beforehand, that there are not going to be any knock-down straightforward arguments on either side.

Philosophy is far from having disproved God, then. We cannot now say with any confidence that there are no possible arguments for the existence of God. Such arguments are being propounded and seriously discussed again. And it is recognised very widely that religious faith may be rational, even in the absence of the type of argument which would establish God as the apex of a metaphysical scheme. The intellectual climate has changed in philosophy in the last fifty years. It has become more pluralistic, more diverse in its viewpoints and methods. It has become less iconoclastic and less satisfied with apparently simple knock-down arguments. It has become much more aware of the difficult and perplexing nature of some of our most central concepts and beliefs. And it has returned to a serious consideration of the idea of God, as a central and perennially fascinating area for philosophical reflection. Within professional philosophy, Christian belief is no longer on the defensive. It is at the leading edge of new and exciting intellectual debates. Perhaps the average person, or even the average Christian, is not aware that this is the case; most of us still seem to be stuck with the problems of thirty or forty years ago, as though they had not been resoundingly refuted.

Philosophy is a difficult and technical subject; it has become even more so in recent years, which is why the best British philosophers are virtually unknown to the British public. But even a short examination of the work of leading philosophers shows the falsity of the opinion that belief in God has lost intellectual credibility. On the contrary, it is now seen to be no less credible, in general, than any other general view of the world; though of course it is no less problematic either. When so many of the Chairs of Philosophy in Britain are now held by Christians, we may well think that the tide has turned, and Christians need have no feeling that they are fighting against the stream.

But, while it is important, intellectual debate is not everything; and it may be felt that the main problems with religion are more practical, centred on everyday life and conduct. Has Christian morality not been shown to be repressive and authoritarian? That is the question we must now face.

Chapter Four

ESCAPE FROM THE NURSERY

Some of the strongest objections people have to religious, and specifically Christian beliefs, are on moral grounds. They have seen Christian moral teaching as infantile and irrational. 'The charge that Christian morality is childish or infantile is an accusation that I think has to be taken very seriously,' Richard Harries, Dean of King's College, London, and a specialist in Christian ethics, says. 'The fact of the matter is that a lot of people have a kind of caricature in their minds of God as a kind of regimental sergeant major, writ large, giving out his orders to mankind which we just have to look up in a book to find out what to do. That is, of course, a gross caricature. Because first of all, although doing the will of God is at the heart of Christian ethics, discovering what the will of God may be is really rather a difficult task. Christians trying to discover what the will of God is put just as much of themselves into it as an agnostic does trying to discover what the right thing to do is. Nevertheless, I think there is a very important difference between a believer's ethics and an unbeliever's ethics. They work with a rather different understanding of what it is to be mature. Obviously a Christian understanding of maturity differs from that of a person who doesn't believe in God. For an agnostic, being mature means simply standing on one's own feet. But for a Christian, being mature means taking responsibility for your life before God and under God.'

That does mean, though, that in one sense, Christians remain children – indeed, they are called children of God. So they are never really in full control of their destinies or truly free from the divine overseer in the sky. Harries again: 'People are meant to remain children of God in the sense that they are dependent upon God moment by moment for their being. They're not immature in the sense of a child failing to grow up. They are dependent upon God in the same way that we are dependent upon the air which we breathe and on the ground upon which we walk. In a similar way, everything is ultimately dependent upon God. And to pray to God, to ask his help, to ask for his guidance, is simply an acknowledgement of his reality.'

Dependence on God may not after all reduce us to the status of perpetual infants, safe in the arms of Jesus. But how are we to go about discovering the will of God? That problem seems almost impenetrably obscure to many people. Richard Harries, however, has a fairly straightforward approach to it: 'First, one has to think hard. A lot of people believe you can look it up in a rule-book, or that if you pray you will get ticker-tape guidance. But on the contrary, one has to think hard about what is going to be in the best interests of oneself and other people. One also needs what the Christian church calls grace, help – first of all, to have a basic sympathy for other people, to want to do the right thing; and secondly, to be able to do it. I don't think the Christian ethic is based simply upon the Bible; it's based on the common-sense morality, the basic moral thinking of ordinary decent people. Naturally, one also has to take into account the very long tradition of Christian wisdom on controversial issues. For instance, there is nearly two thousand years of hard Christian thinking about just and unjust wars or revolutions. But in the end one has to make one's own conscientious decision.'

It is much too simple a view to think that Christians can just look in the Bible to find the answers to their moral problems. For a start, most modern moral issues are not even mentioned there – one will be hard put to it to find anything about abortion, contraception, nuclear disarmament, economic policy or euthanasia. More importantly, if you try to take sentences out of the Bible and apply them literally today, you will soon get in a terrible mess. You will have not only to condemn homosexuals, but stone them to death. You might have to try to exterminate any remaining Amalekites. And you might have to begin having animal sacrifices again. Now the Jews, who do try to keep the Old Testament Law, the Torah, if they are Orthodox, have ways of dealing with these problems. For they have a continuing Rabbinic tradition which can say how the rules are to be applied in new situations. But Christians do not have that advantage; they seem to be stuck with the laws in their original form. This fact has been the cause of continual disputes among Christians, as to how much of the Torah remains relevant today. Only one thing is clear – that the laws as written in the Bible cannot be applied in their original form. Huge problems of interpretation remain.

Some Christians tend to rely on the words of St Paul, that 'Christ is the end of the Law' (Romans, 10,4). They emphasise that the written word kills, but the Spirit gives life; so that we are no longer bound by the written laws at all. Rather, we must look to the present guidance of the Holy Spirit and try to model ourselves on Christ. Revelation, for them, will not consist in particular laws in the Bible, but in an attempt to discern the will of God for our quite new situation. A leading theologian who took this view was Karl Barth; and it is worth noting that he is generally regarded as a very conservative Christian, not some kind of careless radical.

Other Christians will take the written moral rules of the Bible more seriously. But it is generally agreed that it is naive and dangerous to take the rules just as they stand. Rather, one needs to look for more general underlying principles which can be applied in the contemporary world. Again, then, revelation is not just a reading-off of the rules from a clear text. On the contrary, it is vital to try to understand the text in its context, in the context of the Biblical writings as a whole, and in the light of the full revelation of God believed to have been given in Christ. After that, it is important to discern the underlying principle which is at stake. And then one must reflect on how that principle can be best applied in the very different conditions of the modern world. It is clear that this is an arduous and complex process; and it will inevitably involve arguments between people who sincerely interpret the texts in different ways. What this means is that even the person who takes the Biblical texts with full seriousness is going to have to put a lot of thought and reflection into any attempt to discern the will of God. It requires sensitivity, experience and maturity. It is never going to be beyond dispute. So a Christian can believe that the nature of God has been revealed in the Bible. One can believe that it is very important to reflect prayerfully on this revelation as one tries to make moral decisions. But one cannot avoid the conclusion that one has to make the moral decisions oneself, in the end. The Bible gives guidelines; it provides insights and disclosures which can widen our vision and understanding. But it does not take away the need for thought. It does not deprive us of the responsibility for making moral decisions. In short, it should guide us towards maturity; or, as the letter to the Ephesians puts it, build us up until we 'become mature, attaining to the whole measure of the fulness of Christ' (Ephesians 4,13).

So far are we from having a divine rule-book that some Christians would say that there is really no Christian morality at all, of any distinctive interest. Edward Norman, Dean of Peterhouse, Cambridge, and Lecturer in History at Cambridge University, points out that in recent times morality has been progressively disentangled from Christianity. 'We've just come to the end of a fairly long period in which educated opinion has used Christianity as the vehicle of its moral seriousness. We have discovered, within the last 150 years or so, that established opinion has moved away to a series of alternatives, most obviously a set of half-coherent, half-incoherent sacral norms of its own, which I can only describe as a sort of secular humanism. Today, most people have adopted a sort of vicarious substitute Christianity, which depends upon a sort of calculated hedonism. The desire to be moral has become secularised.' One might say that we have at last succumbed to the classical English heresy – the belief that as long as you do good, or don't do too much harm, you will get to heaven; and that is what Christian belief fundamentally consists in.

There is nothing wrong, of course, with doing good. 'Any kind of Christianity worth listenting to is going to be concerned with love of neighbour. But I do think that if motivation for love of neighbour becomes based on alternatives to Christianity, then it ceases to have its moral content in Christianity. My sorrow is that it seems that many leaders of Christian and church opinion identify their Christianity with precisely the same kind of humanism. Yet that is not actually the genius of Christianity, either morally speaking or as a religious system – Christianity should be something that speaks of the transcendent.' Dr Norman is concerned that Christianity should not be identified with a system of morals. 'Religion is something that hurts people in their beings; it's a matter of self-sacrifice. It has to do with giving up a lot of this world's priorities, to find some intimation of lasting and eternal truths.' What is commonly *called* Christian morality is 'the common morality of the ancient world, slightly revised. I don't think there's anything important about Christian morality which differs greatly from the kinds of morality that were available in the ancient world. And much of what is now taken to be Christian morality is anyway tempered by association with Greek ideas.'

Dr Norman is thus very sceptical about the existence of an identifiable 'Christian morality'. 'What's happened is that in British society for many centuries, Christianity has filled a kind of slot for moralising. I don't believe that society was more Christian as a consequence because I don't think Christianity is compatible with the kind of goals people seek through moral codes in society. If I look at the past history of Britain, I perceive that most people have not been particularly religious. What's happened recently is the departure of established opinion from using Christianity as a moral norm; but this has left things more or less where they were before.' What Dr Norman means by morality, it is clear, is those norms which enable people to live together in society in a relatively stable way. He absolutely refuses to identify Christianity with those norms and values which we may call 'ordinary moral seriousness'. 'There is coming to pass a new humanistic Christianity, lacking transcendent qualities, but coinciding almost exactly with the widely diffused, but not particularly Christian, desire to do good.' At the same time, he has a rather definite view that there is a distinctive Christian way of life. 'Where things become so bland and so humanistic that people agree about what's good for humanity, then it seems to me that the fungus of decay is beginning to spread in the system.'

So Christians do have a distinctive view of what is good for humanity. He says: 'Christianity is asking us to accept that the material things among which we move in our lives, and which therefore have moral value for us, are nevertheless only pointers to something else. The world really does mirror and shadow eternity. Above all, Christianity is an encounter with a person whose life was not defined by morality: who came to force us out of this world into seeing that human life has a destiny beyond the immediate and the material and the moral.' The clue to what Dr Norman is saying is that what he terms 'morality' is a matter of this-worldly concerns, of maximising material benefits or ensuring social stability, of making the secular world work. Religion, or at least true religion, when it is not captivated by the world in which it is placed, always seeks to show a vision of a world beyond, which makes material concerns of little interest. It is hardly surprising, then, that he should not be concerned with an alleged Christian morality, which he would see as a captivation of the church by the world. Nevertheless, he is very much concerned with that vision of eternity which is bound to place before us a transcendent goal and a personal ideal of union with the Eternal, albeit by grace and not by virtue of good works.

There is indeed an important part of Christian tradition which is opposed to moralism, to the thought that doing good is the chief end of life and the chief test of its worth. And some of the moralism that has existed in the church in the past has been an instrument of authoritarian repression of individuality. Richard Harries comments: 'I think in the past Christianity has indeed been authoritarian and repressive. It's been psychologically and politically repressive. One of the insights Christians this century have learned from people like Freud and from novelists like D. H. Lawrence is to examine the way in which Christianity has been psychologically repressive. If I may just take one example, D. H. Lawrence had a love-hate relationship with traditional Christian virtues; he wrote poems attacking self-sacrifice and humility. But at the end of those poems he comes to an understanding of these virtues which is quintessentially Christian. So I think that a person like D. H. Lawrence, in attacking the repressive nature of Christianity, actually did Christianity a service, because it cut away all the misinterpretations and caricatures and revealed for us again what true Christian virtue is.'

Richard Harries agrees with Edward Norman about the priority of belief over morality. What is most fundamental is the reality of God; and in the light of the reality of God the whole of human life and what it is to be good does look different. What follows from belief, he thinks, is something rather general; not so much specific rules. 'The first implication of believing in God is that creation is good, that life itself is good, and is to be affirmed; that all aspects of nature are to be affirmed. This has a great deal to say to those, for example, who are concerned to conserve the environment. The Christian faith has a great deal to say, also, about the fundamental goodness of our physical being. It reminds us also, however, that there is a dark side to human life. One of my great heroes, Reinhold Niebuhr, said that Christian ethics reminds us that we are crucifiers of Christ as well as being made in his image. I don't think we can have a realistic approach to human life unless we take both of those truths into account at the same time.'

There is a way of seeing things, a set of basic attitudes, a conception, in Norman's words, of 'what is good for humanity' which is, in the end, rather distinctive. All human beings, whether they believe in God or not, are capable of understanding on fundamental things what is right and what is wrong. It's quite obvious that there have been some extraordinarily good people who have had no religious beliefs at all. But as a Christian one's whole understanding of right and wrong becomes coloured and shaped by one's overall religious view of the world. One thing such an understanding does, in fact, is to undermine confident judgements about good and evil, not make them more certain and definite, as Harries points out: 'Good and evil are much more closely intermingled than a simplistic moralism allows. The poet Robert Browning once wrote some lines that Graham Greene takes as his motto: "My interest is in the dangerous edge of things." Browning goes on to describe the pure prostitute and the good thief. And in Greene's novels one's whole understanding of what is really good is profound and much more true to reality than a sort of simplistic English moralism.'

A rather different picture of Christian morality thus emerges than that of some set of clear and authoritarian rules for moral babes in arms. Morality itself is something deeply problematic. This insight is, as Dr Norman says, true to the inner teaching of faith, which is, after all, that one is saved by faith, not works. But this is often lost sight of by those who seek to draw up definite and absolute sets of moral rules to cover all occasions. Norman fears that the churches are in danger of being taken over by a sort of social gospel, a moralising of faith, a secularisation and domestication of eternity. But this is not really a new problem, and the churches have long interested themselves in the morals of their flocks, and of others, too. Perhaps, in the popular mind at any rate, the church which seems in most danger of authoritarian attitudes to morality is the Roman Catholic, with its claim to a teaching authority in ethics, and its laying down of rules on authority. But there, too, things have changed vastly in recent years. Fr Gerry Hughes, a Jesuit from Heythrop College, London, and author of *Authority in Morals*, presents a view from within the Catholic Church which may surprise many (including several Catholics, I suspect).

'To some extent it was true that, at least in the Catholic Church, many people were encouraged simply to take positions which were given to them as though that was the end of all possible discussion and thought. And to some extent, you will always find that there are people who prefer to be told reasonable answers rather than to think them out for themselves. I would have thought, though, that in more recent years, Catholics have been much more interested in discussing moral problems and discussing them publicly; I think that is especially true in this country. The result of that has been a great ferment of discussion on a very broad range of issues. Nowadays, bishops' conferences, and perhaps the Synod of Bishops as a whole, are much more likely to produce discussion documents which they would hope would further discussion rather than put an end to it. Now you will find some Catholics who will say this is a very bad development; it leads to uncertainty. You will find other Catholics who would very much welcome it. There is no one version of this, I think, currently in the Catholic Church.'

This does not match the popular image of a group of anonymous men in the Vatican, laying down the law about morality from on high. In fact, Gerry Hughes points out that the Catholic Church has issued very few infallible utterances on morality: 'I can't think of any very specific infallible utterance by a Pope on a moral issue. I suppose that, in general, the church would certainly want to teach the importance of forgiveness, of reconciliation, of human rights, but those are very general statements. When they are made specific to highly particular situations – the use of violence when one is oppressed, the rights of the unborn – there is obviously room for considerable disagreement. The church tries to lead people to reflect on that in the light of their Christian tradition. Very occasionally it makes remarks to the effect that it doesn't think that this is a profitable line to pursue; and these are themselves variously received. The church is an institution which seeks to guide or give advice, rather than one which lays down the law. There are some issues – for example, contraception or abortion – on which there is official, though not infallible, Catholic teaching. But this teaching has changed over the centuries in various respects; and is still a matter for considerable debate among Catholics. Some people think this is a good thing; some think it is a bad thing. The fact of the matter is that's what's happened. There are different views of the authoritativeness of the church; but it is uncontroversial that conscientious Catholics can and do disagree about matters like contraception.'

Fr Hughes admits that his view is not going to be universally accepted within the Catholic Church; that tradition has its authoritarians, like any other. But he is not some isolated radical. He is part of the British Catholic tradition in ethical thought, and one of its most respected representatives. And so the view he presents is of particular importance, in seeing how there has been a change in this century in the style of authority even in the Roman Church; in the acceptance of a legitimate plurality, within certain rather broad limits, on moral issues, among Christians. Nor should this really be very surprising. For the Catholic tradition in ethics claims largely to be based, not on revelation, but on reason. And the amount of agreement reason can bring about is rather limited, on specific issues. This appeal to reason is traditionally called the appeal to Natural Law.

'The Natural Law tradition,' Fr Hughes says, 'has got two main strands to it. The first is that what human beings ought to do is to some extent determined by the kind of things that human beings are. Secondly, one can reflect on the kind of things that human beings are by using our God-given minds, and without specifically appealing to revelation in the Scriptures. A lot of philosophers would have thought this was a non-starter some years ago, partly for technical reasons; but partly because, in the case of Catholics, the Natural Law tradition had become very fossilised. Nowadays, we are much more alive to the enormous variety of human lives, that work very well in different sorts of cultures. There are many viable ways of being a good human being, and therefore no one simple ethic you can derive from that. I think that is a very positive step, which goes a long way to rehabilitate what I think is essential to any moral philosophy – that you actually think about human beings and look at the kind of things they are. You can study the needs that human beings have, the ways in which these needs are satisfied in a variety of cultures. You can build up a picture about what kind of life a human being will find satisfying; and therefore, what kind of life we ought to help to promote, and assist other people to live. That is what I take the basis of any Natural Law morality to be; and it has always been said to be the basis of Catholic ethics.'

The ancient Christian tradition of Natural Law is in fact making a remarkable comeback in general moral philosophy, which parallels the return to metaphysics which was noted in the previous chapter. Whereas philosophers like Ayer held that ethics was almost entirely a matter of the emotions, a subjective matter of preference, there is a recovery of belief in some objective basis for morality among philosophers today. Renford Bambrough, Alisdair MacIntyre, John Lucas, Geoffrey Warnock and Philippa Foot are all leading moral philosophers in the British tradition who have argued strongly in recent years that ethics should be rooted in a view of human nature, and that an objective morality can be founded in some way on a study of human needs and interests, of what enables human beings to flourish. But this is not a return to an authoritarian and monolithic system of rules. Largely in the light of the strong criticisms of Nietzsche and the insights of Freud and behavioural psychologists, moralists have had to go back to the roots of the Western ethical tradition; and Christians have rediscovered that their tradition is in fact more open and creative than the pedantic scholastic edifices which had been built on them over the centuries would suggest. The things that make for human enrichment, for human flourishing, may take a number of forms; and it is wrong to be too restrictive about the possible forms it may yet take.

This openness to plurality may seem very unsettling; but in fact it is not at all new in Christian history. It would be a very myopic view which thought that moral disputes were something new in the Christian tradition. Disputes are an inevitable part of any tradition which places an emphasis on rational investigation. Charles Elliott, at one time Director of Christian Aid: 'We need to remember that in any century you have had a range of opinions within the Christian church. In the last century, for instance, you had Christian socialists, people campaigning for improved factory conditions, for the ten-hour working day and so on. And you had people claiming that socialism was incompatible with Christianity. We've always had this tension. I am not sure that the dynamics of the tension have changed all that much this century. But it is an illogical argument that because there are differences, then Christianity has nothing to say. What is perhaps becoming clearer in this century is that we have to relate theological method much more to the context in which people live, suffer and die. It seems to me that the liberation theologians and perhaps the feminist theologians in the United States and Europe, are telling us that we have got to look at where people are, what makes them as they are, and do our theology from that starting point. Out of that will come fresh moral and political insights. I think that is a very liberating way of going about it, though it does lead to confusion and muddle. That is something we have got to learn to live with.'

For Elliott, Christianity has a much greater cutting-edge in social and political issues than it would have, for instance, for Dr Norman; indeed, he might be thought to be just one of those moralisers of faith against whom Dr Norman warns us. But this turns out to be a very complicated issue. It is, as has just been seen, part of the Christian tradition to found morality on a perception of what enables a full humanity to flourish. And, while it may be a bit difficult to say precisely what full human flourishing would consist in, it is at least obvious that many people in today's world have no chance of flourishing at all. Elliott again: 'People in Britain, by and large, have not experienced terror and repression, such as people in Central America, Brazil, Chile and the Philippines have experienced it. Those are exactly the countries where liberation theology is alive and well. It is changing people and changing churches. What it is basically about is seeing the story of the Exodus, the liberation of the Jews from slavery and oppression in Egypt, as in some sense the type, the essence, of the whole Biblical record – including the life, death and resurrection of Jesus Christ. What this means is that the purpose of religion becomes identified with freeing people from everything that diminishes them, everything that makes them less than fully human. This has to be worked out in the political domain; but it has also to be worked out in the spiritual domain. Liberation theology is precisely about holding those two domains together in a creative tension. Obviously it implies confronting all evil and corrupt and dehumanising civil powers.'

Liberation theology is a movement which originated in Latin America in 1967. It is, as Dr Elliott points out, based on an emphasis on the Biblical theme of liberation – liberation from Egypt, from exile in Babylon, from Roman oppression. Jesus is spoken of as the redeemer, the liberator; so liberation is a central theme in the Bible, without a doubt. Liberation theologians would not want to deny that the primary meaning of liberation must be liberation from sin, so as to be freely related to God. But they would point out that the Bible nowhere opposes the material to the spiritual, as though one was evil and the other good. The prophets call for justice in society, and they look for a real political freedom from oppression. It may be true that Jesus' Kingdom is not of this world; but Christians still pray that it should be realised on earth. And so they should clearly work for it, if it is at all possible. Just as the Salvation Army has long said that you must first feed people, before you can preach the Gospel to them; so the liberation theologians say that people must be freed from political tyranny and oppression, in the name of Christ.

The stress on the importance of political freedom is also implicit in the recovery of the Natural Law tradition; it does not depend wholly on Biblical revelation. For if Natural Law requires us to consider what will most satisfy human needs, it must call us to give people the freedom to meet their needs. What underlies Natural Law is the belief that God has created human beings for a purpose; and, indeed, that he has given to each one a unique and individual value and destiny. So we are bound to seek to create social conditions which will best help people to fulfil their God-given purpose. And that again requires freedom and a sort of society in which each individual has a chance to realise his or her purpose. Of course that purpose cannot consist just in the accumulation of material goods. It must in the end, for a Christian, be the spiritual purpose of relationship to God. But that does at least require the condemnation of any State system which so oppresses people that they find such a relationship very hard to find; or which denies them fundamental rights to life and a reasonable degree of personal freedom.

These are the things that Dr Elliott stresses; and so he represents the other pole from Dr Norman of a tension between a this-worldly view of the Gospel and an other-worldly view of it which runs throughout Christian history. Elliott refuses to say that either is wrong; you must see things from where you are. 'What I find God saying to me and the people among whom I am privileged to work is something about discovering a freedom, both an inner and an outer freedom, in a long and difficult journey. To put that in some kind of a context, I am attached fairly loosely to a congregation in Brixton. We've been through a very difficult period over the last eighteen months.

But I think people in that congregation are talking about hanging on to values of reconciliation, balancing them with values of justice. The task of Christian morality is working that out in a very polarised situation, trying to find the way that leads to a full humanity and a full sense of freedom.'

We return yet again to these words 'full humanity' and 'inner freedom'. And it is easy to see how, in specific social contexts, they can come to take the form of a protest against dehumanising conditions of life. Yet it may rightly be asked, if that is what Christianity is really about, how does it differ from humanism? Is it not Marx who has made this way of thinking fashionable, after all? There is some truth in that; though it may be asked in return how much Marx took from the prophetic tradition in Judaism and Christianity, and how far the church in his day had strayed from the gospel ideals preached by Jesus. 'I think it is true that Christianity was authoritarian in the past. People took it for granted that absolute monarchy was the normal form of government on earth and in heaven as well. So God was seen primarily as the all-powerful rewarder and punisher and controller of events. Obviously Christianity has changed a lot since the time of the French Revolution. I don't think now it has that aspect at all. In many countries, Christianity functions as a protest against the established order. You can see, in countries like Poland, how very creative it can be in this role.' The words are those of Don Cupitt, Dean of Emmanuel College, Cambridge, and well-known critic of many of our traditional ways of talking about God. I do not myself agree with all that he says about God, but he has a strong positive point to make about the moral and spiritual goals which are to be found in the Christian faith.

'Religion provides a background framework conception of human life. We tend to create a hierarchical vision of the world with ourselves near the top; we try to consolidate ourselves, to defend our own egos. The Gospel is a protest against this power-centred, hierarchical vision that we tend to generate. It is a way of self-surrender, renunciation, of learning to accept that, as individuals, we are not the only pebble on the beach. It is trying to find a new posture in the face of the mystery of the human condition. That does mean accepting self-loss, finding a basic spiritual poise in life. I do not want to say that mysticism or religious experience open up a pathway to an entirely separate supernatural realm. I believe that spirituality, spiritual discipline, is necessary to us to live well in this world.'

Here again one can see a difference of emphasis from Dr Norman; for Don Cupitt, what happens in this world is of primary importance. We cannot be content just to negate its aspirations and desires. We must seek to transform them. It seems that one of the most important insights Christian morality has rediscovered in this century is the spiritual importance of the material world. It is not a wholly other-worldly faith, leaving matter wholly unredeemed. And it is not a wholly this-worldly faith, leaving matter without hope of redemption. It is a way of seeing the spiritual reality within this world, of discerning a true incarnation of spirit in the physical and moral worlds.

'In religion you have a huge body of symbols, stories and ritual practices, which communicate to us religious values,' Don Cupitt holds. 'In the Christian symbols about Jesus one sees the pattern of suffering and glory. He exists in two states, one in which he is afflicted and one in which he is triumphant. So when we see our fellow human being oppressed and afflicted, we see Christ in him. And in the glorified Christ we see an image of human liberation. So Christ symbolises human beings both in their state of affliction and in their state of freedom, fulfilment and self-realisation. For me, Christ is a model for Christian ethics, the way we should see our own lives and the way we should treat other people.'

In Cupitt's view, religion provides symbols which open up a special perspective on human life. But that perspective is not given once for all, in a completely unchanging way. It is itself something which modifies as it is perceived in different cultures by people of different temperaments. 'It is obvious historically,' he says, 'that Christianity was very different in the nineteenth century, the sixteenth, the eighteenth. Christians have perceived things very differently, because religion and morality evolve historically.' So the church's task will depend on the particular historical situation in which it finds itself. We have very general values of love, forgiveness and so on; these are delineated for ever in the story of Christ; they cannot change. But the way these are spelled out in particular practices and particular ways of life will differ from one period to another. So he sees Christianity not so much as a given unchanging authoritative system, but rather as a continuing creative task.

More radical Christians, like Don Cupitt himself, will value these Christian symbols for their own sake, without insisting that they have to be tied down to historical events, or grounded in some metaphysical reality. My own view would be that the occurrence of the historical crucifixion and resurrection is important; for if they indeed happened, they show that there is a truly existing God who reveals to us, in these things, the way of life he requires of us and who will bring us to fulfilment in his presence after this earthly life. But I do think Cupitt is entirely right in his portrayal of the Christian way of life as one of self-loss and of a spiritual discipline which has to be worked out in suffering and action in the world, to try to realise true human fulfilment, human flourishing during this life.

This differs from a humanistic morality in two main ways. First, it is a matter of an inward pilgrimage towards a state of love for all things, a turning from ambition and desire for material goods in order to find that paradoxical sort of fulfilment which comes in following the way of the cross. Many humanists would not be able to make any sense of this, and would regard morality as only a matter of helping others, not of pursuing a personal ideal. And second, it has an element of demand and necessity about it – what Cupitt calls the 'religious requirement'. This is not an option, which may or may not be chosen at will. Of course, we can choose it or reject it; but that is not an arbitrary choice. It is a choice which determines the sort of person one is. If one rejects it, one turns away from one's true humanity, from authentic human life. To accept it, on the other hand, is to discover what, at the deepest level, one truly is, and what it is to flourish as a human being.

I think Don Cupitt would say that this is so, whether or not there is a metaphysical, omnipotent, omniscient God who creates the universe. In his more extreme moods, he might even say that the existence of such a God would reduce moral commitment to a matter of prudence, and of obedience to divine commands, and so deprive it of worth. However, if one is careful to have a fully Christian idea of God, this danger is avoided. For the Christian God is one who gives himself to the uttermost in love, as the cross shows. So the appropriate human response to him is not one of craven fear, but of gratitude and love. This is a point which makes an enormous difference to the way one sees morality. It is possible to see one's duty as something to be done for its own sake. This is a

91

stern Stoic attitude, and much to be commended. But while the Christian should not deny that you should do what is right just because it is right, he should not say that this is the only reason you should do what is right. You should *also* do it because God wants you to do it, and you want to do what pleases God.

A faint analogy is with human love. If a man and a woman marry, then there are certain duties each ought to carry out. The man ought to care for his wife, and he should share in the household chores and the bringing-up of children because it is his duty to do so. Yet if a marriage consists only of duties, there is something wrong with it. It is much better for each person to do something out of love, just because the other would like it done. In a good marriage, you may do something because it is your duty. But you will also do it because your partner would like you to; you do it out of sheer love. And that goes a long way beyond duty, and is somehow not quite so grim and stern. So it is with God. You should certainly keep promises, be faithful, tell the truth and seek justice because it is right to do so. But you can also do these things because you know God would like you to; and out of the sheer love of God. That gives a completely different feel to morality. Indeed, the perfected saint will have transcended duty; he or she will do everything for the love of God; and duty will merely be a reminder of what love will naturally do.

Thus the Christian can transcend duty in the response of love. Moralism is transcended when one sees life as a quest for and a response to the love of God. That makes an enormous difference to what one does in life. Fr Hughes says: 'I would look at the moral life as part of a growth towards God. A humanist would not see that. It is not that I would have a different morality; but I would look at the whole enterprise as the beginning of a pilgrimage that has an end somewhere else. I don't see why a sincere humanist and a sincere Christian need to differ in their morality. On the other hand, if I look at you and try to respond to you as a person in whom Christ lives, for whom Christ died, I might not be doing anything different from a humanist, but I would be doing it in a different perspective.'

The Christian should see all other people as objects of God's love and as places wherein God dwells. Thus they become holy; they come to have a special dignity and uniqueness that makes them, in an inviolable sense, sacred. I respond to you with the love I owe to God. And I believe that this love will reach a fruition in a perfected relationship with God, when I see him face to face, and know as I am known. The Christian life has a goal that the atheist cannot have. For an atheist, this life is all there is; and there is no further meaning or purpose to be found than what we can find here. But the Christian will look for the weaving of his strange and obscure life into a meaning and design which will become clear in God, and he will look to its fulfilment in a realm beyond this. It is not a question of 'pie in the sky when you die'. But it is a belief that the strivings and struggles of this life will not be in vain; that they can be brought to good.

As Charles Elliott says: 'Most of us, most of the time, think that we are getting absolutely nowhere, that trying to struggle for a freer, more human world is a waste of time. But we can be nourished in hope, as Christians, even in that situation. What we hope for is the final redemption of the whole created order. So we can never finally despair.' Christianity leads us to go on with hope, yet without demanding that we should see immediate results. It is perhaps only a religious view which can give this firm commitment to social action, which does not despair when it does not get immediate results. Perhaps it is because Marxism has nothing to offer at this point that it commits itself to the way of violence, striving impatiently to bring about by force what it cannot foresee coming by the patience of love. So Marxism destroys that which it most hopes for, instituting a final dictatorship and tyranny in a vain attempt to force into existence a society of freedom and love. Marxism in practice exhibits all the rage and violence of a failure to find immediate Utopia. Christianity contains within itself the resources for a commitment to human good and social justice, without the bitterness that comes from insisting on immediate results.

Finally, Christianity gives moral commitment a depth which atheism does not have available to it. For the humanist, morality must ultimately be a matter of human choice and decision – noble and admirable maybe; but, after all, just a heroic cry against the indifference of the universe. Perhaps that is how it is; and such nobility of spirit may not be mocked; it is too precious and pitiable for that. Yet the Christian, in all conscience, sees more. He sees in moral commitment, in the sense of moral claim and imperative, a pointer to transcendence. He hears there an echo of the voice of God, often unrecognised yet undeniable in its power and authority. In the face of such a claim, he can only say, if he is true to himself: 'Here I stand: I can no other.' And, the Christian will say, by that utterance he acknowledges God, an authority greater than self, by which the self is judged.

So, in the early years of this century, it looked as if Christian morality was finished – exposed as infantile, repressive and irrational, trying to impose arbitrary rules on an uncritical flock of retarded sheep. Things look quite different now. Christians throughout the world are actively involved, and are sometimes the only guardians of, movements for peace and justice. They are strong in proclaiming the importance of human rights, political freedom and responsible care of the environment. Christians have learned much from their critics, from Freud and Marx and Lawrence; and in consequence have been driven back to a thorough-going reappraisal of their own tradition. The quest, it is agreed, is for human flourishing, not repression. And it is becoming apparent to more people now that such a quest needs to be supported by an underlying vision of the way things are. We should not ever support Christianity just because it will help us to survive in a depressing world. But our sense of moral claim and of the objective rootedness of morality in the way things are is in itself a pointer to the reality of God – the God who revealed himself to the prophets of Israel primarily as the one who demanded justice and promised the ultimate victory of his Kingdom of peace. Christianity calls for the transformation of the material world to enable all created life to be enriched and fulfilled. It also cherishes the inward quest for union with the Eternal which is at the heart of true religion. It holds these two things together in a creative tension, so that, at its best, it avoids both a world renouncing quietism and a continually restless social activism. Seen in this way, the moral strength and appeal of Christianity may be stronger now than it has seemed for many years.

Chapter Five

WHATEVER HAPPENED TO JESUS?

Was Jesus a deluded prophet who lived on magic mushrooms in a cave in Galilee? Did he try to start a revolt against the Roman Empire; and after surviving an unsuccessful attempt to crucify him, go to live in France, or perhaps in Pakistan, and raise a family with Mary Magdalen? Fantastic as it may seem, this is the picture of Jesus you might get from some of the books and television programmes that have recently hit the headlines. It must look as if the Bible has been left in tatters by the scholars, who have researched away like bookworms, destroying everything as they chew their way through the text, until virtually nothing is left. Talking to scientists and philosophers, I have found among many of them a much more positive attitude to and greater respect for religious beliefs than the popular image often suggests. Christian morality, too, seems to have found a new lease of life in its recovery of a basic belief in human dignity and freedom, and its attempt to shed old authoritarian attitudes. But all this is to no avail for Christians if it turns out that Jesus himself has completely disappeared from view, that the Gospels are completely unreliable, so that the Christian faith is nothing more than a collection of myths and legends.

It is important, then, to ask just how things stand in Biblical scholarship, and here again there does seem to be quite a gulf between how things are popularly perceived, both by Christians and by non-Christians, and how they really are. A popular view is that Biblical criticism has wholly destroyed any confidence we can have in the Bible; and so it has undermined faith. People both inside and outside the churches see the scholars as the enemy. One reason for this is pointed out by Morna Hooker, Lady Margaret Professor of Divinity in the University of Cambridge. 'Part of our problem is that there has been a great crisis. People have been brought up to look at the New Testament in a particular way, which is a hangover from a past age. For centuries, the Gospels were treated as historical records of what happened, exactly as it happened. There has been a revolution in our understanding of the nature of the Gospels. We've come to realise that this is not the way in which we handle any other document from the past; and the Gospels themselves are products in which are blended facts and interpretations of what people remembered about Jesus, stories which had been told and retold, passed on and preached on.'

In a sense, as Morna Hooker says, what we have got in the Gospels is a whole lot of stories which have been interpreted already by faith, which are in some sense sermons in their own right. They are attempting to get across to their readers their understanding of what the Gospel about Jesus Christ is. This way of looking at the Gospels can at first be a great shock to many church-goers who have not been trained to think of them in this way. It seems as if the ground is being knocked away; as though we are being told, 'We can't be sure what Jesus said.' Words have been altered; things have been added; differing accounts of the same story within the Gospels seem to be conflicting. 'The moment you sit down and look at the Gospels and realise that the same story is being told by different evangelists from a different point of view, you see that you have not got actual records of what happened. You have got stories used in order to proclaim the Gospel. When you realise that, far from the ground being knocked from under your feet, you realise that what you are being given is a whole wealth of interpretation, as people have tried to come to terms with their experience of Jesus, to express it and understand their new faith in what God has been doing through Jesus.'

Once you start looking at the Gospels in this way, you realise that you are being offered something which is rich, vibrant and alive, the proclamation of the Gospel in different situations; how it was preached to different communities at different times. This is part of the richness which has come out of recent studies of the gospels. We are much more aware of the different ways in which the four evangelists have understood the message of Jesus. 'In the past, we have tried to put all four Gospels together; people have not bothered very much whether something came from Matthew or John. Now we are much more interested in the different ways the evangelists were preaching the Gospel in their own communities. There is a unity in their understanding of the Gospel, and yet each is interpreting it from his own point of view, seeing how it is living for him. That is an enormous richness which has come from modern study of the Gospels.'

People can find it hard to escape from the belief that every word of the Gospels is dictated by God, so that it must be right in every detail. This view of revelation is found in many religions; Muslims have believed it about the Koran; orthodox Hindus have believed it about the Veda; orthodox Jews have said that even the size and order of the letters in the Hebrew script is divinely appointed. But such a view has not been part of orthodox Christian faith; and, as Hooker points out, once you see what the Gospels really are – that they are attempts to bring out the *meaning* of Jesus' life for their readers – the temptation to see them as infallible biographies begins to fade. There are so many things we do not know about Jesus – how tall he was, what colour his hair was, whether he had a beard (he didn't, in the earliest paintings; but he has done ever since), what he did for most of his life – we just don't have a biography. The gospel writers were not concerned with that; they wanted to preach a living Lord, by bringing out what he had meant to them or to those who had known him as their teacher, but they were in no doubt that he had existed, and had said and done certain things. And they did mean to record those things, even if they wanted to interpret them at the same time. New Testament scholars seem to be rather more confident now than they were in the early years of this century that we can recover something of Jesus from these records; though of course there is not unanimity among them.

The range of belief between those who feel there is very little one can state with great certainty about what Jesus was saying and those who feel that much more can be set out is enormous. There is, however, a middle ground which is held by most British scholars; some have remarked that there is now underway a new quest for the historical Jesus. In the nineteenth century, scholars would often try to reconstruct a rather exact picture of what Jesus was like, even down to what he thought and felt as he wandered around the country. This search for the historical Jesus was brought to an end when the famous New Testament scholar Rudolf Bultmann said that he felt you could know virtually nothing about him. Most of Bultmann's major work was done in the 1940s. Because he thought that the 'scientific world-view' excluded the occurrence of miracles, he saw most of the events recorded in the Gospels as legends or

97

myths. His views came to have great authority, because the scholarship of his textual analysis and historical research was exemplary. Since that time, however, there has been a reaction against his extreme historical scepticism. Perhaps miracles cannot be ruled out by definition; and it has to be admitted that the Gospels are amongst the best historical records we have from that era. So a renewed search for the historical Jesus has begun.

The search today is, however, much more tentative in its approach and in its conclusions than the original quest was. It could be compared to building up an impressionist picture. One might be uncertain about particular incidents and sayings, but nevertheless feel that there is enough evidence in the Gospels to suggest that Jesus must have said and done something rather like this. Even though we cannot be sure of the precise words or of the exact details of the incidents, we can say fairly confidently that Jesus spoke about the Kingdom of God, that he healed, taught in parables, acted with tremendous authority and so on.

Nowadays it is realised that Gospel criticism is rather like an archaeological dig. 'You have to begin with the top layer,' Morna Hooker says, 'that is what we have in the Gospels.' The first task is to look at the Gospels and see what each evangelist is trying to do and how his interests and emphases have shaped his handling of the material. Then in the Gospels you find there are individual stories, which are common to the evangelists, so you can dig a little lower, and ask questions about the stories as they were shaped by the community and the beliefs of those who handled the material before it came to the evangelists. Beyond that, at the bottom layer, there is clearly Jesus himself. But does that mean that *he* is almost wholly hidden from view? Strangely enough, recent discoveries have shed much new light on the person of Jesus and the social context in which he lived. The most important of these has undoubtedly been the discovery of the Dead Sea scrolls.

Geza Vermes, Reader in Jewish Studies at the University of Oxford, summarises the significance the scrolls have had in bringing new focus to the world in which the Gospels were created, on the religious practices, the concerns, the general civilisation of the people among whom Jesus was born, and the ideas of which Jesus expressed and passed on to his disciples, so that it is possible to ask how Jesus fits into this general picture. 'Until the mid twentieth century, the documents on which the knowledge of Judaism was based were considerably more recent than the period of the New Testament. This was the first time that Jewish writings belonging to the so-called intertestamental era, between 200 BC and 100 AD, first became available to scholarship. The Dead Sea scrolls represent the writings and preoccupations, the ideas of a religious community which considered itself separate from the main body of Judaism, the representative of the ultimate revelation of God. Their master, the "Teacher of Righteousness", was seen as someone who was able to convey to his disciples the real religious truth. From this point of view, the Dead Sea community presents an exact parallel to the movement that followed Jesus after his death and disappearance from the historical world. Consequently, we not only have documents which belong to the period. We also have a movement which I would imagine presents the best comparative source for the understanding of early Christianity as a religious current. I would, however, be totally unwilling to connect the two movements. I do not believe that the connection is anything other than historical parallelism.'

From the Scrolls you find that there were religious groups which considered themselves the only representatives of the revelation of God. But the Teacher of Righteousness was not the same type of religious teacher as Jesus of Nazareth. For one thing, the Teacher of Righteousness appears to have been a priest, which Jesus was not. Secondly, his concerns were probably more doctrinal, more technical than those of Jesus, who was primarily a teacher of the simple, the uneducated. This is partly due to the fact that Jesus came from Galilee, which was not one of the great centres of learning in ancient Judaism. On the contrary, Jesus was himself a countryman who felt at home in the villages and the small towns of the lakeside of Galilee; he was unaccustomed to the life and the way of thinking of people in the cities and in particular in Jerusalem. 'If you want to characterise Jesus on the basis of the Gospels,' Dr Vermes concludes, 'and as contrasted with the Teacher of Righteousness, he was essentially an itinerant preacher among the simple country people of Galilee. He was also a healer and an exorcist, a charismatic teacher whose main task was to prepare and introduce the Kingdom of God, which people expected very anxiously in those days.'

A definite picture of Jesus as a historical figure has emerged; and this might seem rather surprising because Dr Vermes is a specialist in Jewish studies, with no Christian axe to grind. His works, notably perhaps *Jesus the Jew*, have revolutionised many Christian views of Jesus, by showing more of the Jewish context within which he lived and taught, and so increasing our understanding of his essential Jewishness. We can warm to this picture of the charismatic prophet and healer; and see him, not as some supernatural spaceman dropped into Galilee by accident, as it were; but as a devout Jew who felt God's call to proclaim the coming of the Kingdom. It is ironic that it was a radical Christian theologian, Rudolf Bultmann, who said we could have no knowledge of Jesus and it is an eminent Jewish scholar, Geza Vermes, who is suggesting that we can *have* reliable historical knowledge of him.

Some Christian scholars are probably right, that the gospels were not meant to describe precisely the life and actions of an individual. They were meant to provide a description of the message of Jesus in the framework of his life-story. On the other hand, the very fact that the writers of the Gospels opted for a biographical framework indicates that they had some interest in this. Otherwise, they could have presented the teaching of Jesus without connecting it with the events of his life. The letters of Paul hardly ever refer to anything connected with the life of Jesus. The teaching presented by Paul has no biographical context. The Gospel writers do provide at least a minimal amount of historical references concerning the age in which Jesus was born and lived. We know that it was somewhere at the end of the reign of Herod; we know that he was crucified under Pontius Pilate, who was prefect of Judaea between 26 and 36 AD; that most of his activity occurred in Galilee, a province with its own Herodian ruler, Herod Antipas, and not under direct Roman administration as was the case in Judaea. 'By collecting all these historical and sociological data and comparing them with the hints in the Gospels,' Dr Vermes says, 'I believe one can obtain a fairly clear though not very detailed picture of Jesus. Consequently, in this respect I think I am considerably more optimistic and positive than many Christian New Testament scholars have been.'

Perhaps we can, without unduly forcing the evidence, see the same sort of swing in Biblical criticism that we have seen in science, philosophy and ethics. Starting from a rather dogmatic and authoritarian picture, where every word ascribed to Jesus had to be true, exactly as stated (even though he probably spoke Aramaic, and the New Testament was written in Greek); things moved rapidly to a very radical position, where we were said to know nothing at all about Jesus, or where the wildest theories were just as plausible as the traditional ones. But more recently there has been a return to a position where we neither have to take as literal truth every word ascribed to Jesus, nor reject all of them as legendary, but where we can get a clear, if impressionist picture of Jesus. Graham Stanton, Professor of New Testament Studies at King's College, London, thinks this marks a fairly pronounced movement of thought in Biblical studies.

'Over the last twenty years or so there has been quite a significant change within Biblical scholarship, and in particular in the study of the Gospels. On the whole, there is now more agreement than there was that we have a fairly reliable portrait of Jesus of Nazareth in our Gospels. Roman Catholics, conservative evangelicals and scholars who would make no particular religious claims, do agree on the general reliability of the portrait of Jesus. Certainly, the more extreme and sceptical views of the historicity of Jesus are now out of fashion. Just as a tiny illustration of that, even in the Soviet Union, the standard Soviet Encyclopedias now accept that Jesus of Nazareth did exist and was an important Jewish teacher of his time. Twenty or thirty years ago, they simply stated that he was a complete myth and did not exist at all.'

Even though the Gospels are not biographies, but attempts to evoke the meaning of Jesus' life for their readers, we may reasonably accept that they give a picture of a recognisable person. But there remains a major problem. If Christians are people who follow Jesus of Nazareth as their spiritual teacher, they do have to believe that the picture given in the Gospels is reliable. At the moment, everything seems to show that it is. But might evidence not turn up which undermines the picture? Some people were very worried by the Dead Sea scrolls at first, though we can now see that they help us to understand Jesus better. But might some new scrolls not turn up which show that Christian belief is false, after all?

'I would accept that it is theoretically possible that the archaeologists might turn up new evidence or there might be new literary evidence to confirm me, as a historian, in the belief that the Gospels are utterly unreliable, that they come, say, from the fourth century AD and therefore are utterly worthless as historical records. In that remote case, I personally would cease to be a Christian.' So Professor Stanton is fully prepared to let his faith rest on historical probabilities. 'Christianity has always maintained that at the heart of our religion is Jesus of Nazareth, a particular person who lived at a particular point in time in a particular place. If you are convinced that there is no evidence for Jesus at all, or that he was a rogue, Christian faith as I understand it would collapse.'

Christianity is not merely some general doctrine about a timeless God. It says that God acts, and sometimes acts decisively, in history; and that he did so in Jesus. That can never be proved historically, though it can be more or less probable, on the evidence. But is high probability enough for committing one's whole life to its truth? There is general agreement that Jesus was a prophet-figure; that he did most unusual things in his healing actions, that he taught in very striking ways that do not quite fit in with traditional Jewish teaching of the time. One can say a great deal along those lines. But then the question arises, what about the very early Christian claims about Jesus?

There is no doubt that they rest ultimately on belief in the resurrection. Christian and Jewish scholars can agree to a considerable extent on the nature of Jesus' teaching; but Christians go on to claim that in the post-resurrection period, the followers of Jesus developed particular convictions about him in the light of their resurrection-faith. Professor Stanton is unequivocal: 'The resurrection faith is absolutely crucial as far as the development of Christian belief is concerned.' As Professor Hooker puts it, 'We have to remember that all the material we have comes from this side of the resurrection. It has been passed on by those who believe in Jesus as a living Lord. That Jesus has been raised from the dead is the starting-point of those who tell these stories. There is an enormous difference between a Jewish travelling Rabbi and the living Lord and Messiah.' What we have, then, is not a body of neutral evidence upon which we then have to make some sort of decision. What we have is a testimony to a discernment of God in the life of Jesus, as seen in the light of the experience of his resurrection. Professor Stanton again: 'There is no way back from the experience of the apostles, from their beliefs, to the actual history. One can say that there is quite strong historical evidence for the empty tomb. Geza Vermes has argued that the empty tomb tradition is one of the earliest and best attested elements of the Gospels; but that does not *prove* anything. As a Christian, I believe God raised Jesus from the dead; but there are other explanations; perhaps the disciples stole the body. So there is not absolutely certain proof; but one can say as a historian that the faith of the early Christians was an entirely plausible reaction to their experiences of the risen-ness of Jesus. They believed that God had raised Jesus from the dead; and one cannot prove that their belief was correct, any more than one can prove that two young people really are genuinely in love. One can see the results of it; one can say they have been attracted to one another. But one can't go beyond that. So it is with the early followers of Jesus and their faith in him as risen from death.'

The Christian faith would never have got started at all if it had not been for this quite extraordinary belief the apostles had that Jesus, whom they had seen crucified, had been raised from death and had appeared to them. If, as Professor Stanton says, we cannot get back beyond this belief, beyond the experiences of the apostles, it might be suggested that we should just stop there, with their experiences, and not go on to claim anything about actual historical occurrences. But there are two things wrong with that suggestion. First, their experiences, too, are historical occurrences, though of a peculiarly mental kind. You are not really escaping from making historical claims if you commit yourself to the view that a certain group of people really did have such experiences. It can never be more than probably true that they did; history cannot prove that either; so, if your present beliefs depend on that, they are still depending on historical facts. Secondly, what they claimed was that they encountered Jesus alive; their experience was not some purely inner state – or they did not think it was. It was precisely an encounter with the teacher whom they knew to have died. So you cannot make Christian faith somehow more secure if you try to make it depend just on the experiences of the apostles. For you have to believe that those experiences were veridical, if they are to be worth anything. That is, you do have to accept that Jesus manifested himself to them after death. That is where the Christian faith began.

Can one show this to be a plausible claim, one that might be accepted on historical grounds? At this point one must stress that the resurrection is not presented in the Gospels as irrefutable evidence, to any impartial observer, that God has intervened in nature – Jesus did not appear to Pontius Pilate or the High Priest and thus unambiguously declare himself to all. It is presented as a disclosure of God's power to save from evil and death, given to the company of disciples. It is seen primarily as a fulfilment of God's promises to Israel, though it transforms those promises, and the Messianic expectation, in an unforeseen way. And it shows God's final purpose, which is the glorification of humanity by union with him. Thus it has the power to relate the disciples to God in a new way; and in that present power to transform human lives lies its chief significance.

This means that whether or not one believes that the resurrection occurred is not something that will depend on considerations that could be accepted by historians of very differing general views. It will depend upon a great range of other factors, very complex in character and so subtly interwoven with one another that they are enormously difficult to disentangle. For example, the probability that the resurrection occurred will be raised if you believe, on other grounds, that there is a God; that God has a purpose in creating the world; that he sometimes acts in particular ways to forward that purpose and to disclose his nature. The probability will be raised if you think that it fits into a more general pattern of divine activity which seems to provide a good overall explanation of all the available and relevant evidence. It will be raised if one has, in one's own personal experience, a form of knowledge of God which seems to have been mediated through the person of Christ, felt as a living presence; and if one accepts the testimony of the Christian community over the ages that this presence has indeed mediated God to people and reconciled them to God in a new way.

There is a host of factors which need to be considered. The historian can only contribute to one strand of this complex process. He is in no position, purely as a historian, to say whether or not God is to be discerned at work here, any more than a biologist who sticks strictly to the principles of biology is in any position to say that a human personality exists in a certain human organism. The biologist is confined to talking about bones, chemicals and physical structure. And while that may give clues to the person whose body is being thus analysed, it will not conclusively establish that a person exists there at all. So the historian may use all the resources of textual criticism, comparison with social context and with relevantly analogous cases. But in the end, the historian is unable to take a position on whether God is at work here or not; and so the decision must be made on all those other complex grounds I have mentioned.

Does that not mean that the believer and the unbeliever must approach the text with quite different presuppositions, and are bound to come to different conclusions about it? To an extent it does. You cannot avoid bringing your own prior beliefs to the material, and they must affect your assessment of what is likely to have happened.

It is interesting to compare treatments of the person of Jesus which have been given in the cinema or on television in recent years. Some years ago, in the sort of Hollywood treatment favoured by Cecil B. de Mille, a handsome, bearded Jesus strode around, accompanied by a crowd of invisible singing angels at key points, performing miracles in a tasteful and dramatic way and preaching love and peace to all. The demons, the Kingdom of God and the approaching judgement on Jerusalem were rather played down, and no social message was discernible at all. More recently, the fashion has been to portray Jesus as more or less an ordinary man, friend of the unemployed; a down-to-earth, no-nonsense type of person who rubbed the authorities up the wrong way and came to a sticky end. It is noteworthy that there have been few treatments which seriously try to place Jesus in a fully Jewish, Galilean context, and portray him as the utterly charismatic spiritual teacher that he must have been.

I do not want to make any particular point in saying this, except to stress how differing assessments of the person of Jesus, and of the New Testament evidence in general, must reflect differing assessments of how God works in the world now. We are never going to get complete agreement; but that is not unique to the New Testament. It is a feature of all history; and it will naturally loom larger when basic religious beliefs, or the lack of them, is also at issue. The gulf will be greatest between those who take a very conservative attitude to the Bible, believing, perhaps, that it is divinely protected from error, and those who take it as a human record of imperfectly remembered historical occurrences. Yet though such differences will always exist, there are more points of agreement between Biblical scholars of differing religious beliefs than one might suspect; and there is a clearer recognition of the legitimacy of such diverse interpretations than there was.

Dr Dick France is a lecturer at the London Bible College, and a conservative evangelical. He therefore starts with the presupposition that the texts are free from error. For him, the divide between those who are prepared to think of the possibility that Jesus was something other than just a man, albeit a man very close to God, and those who will not look beyond the purely human perspective, is a radical philosophical difference, which affects the whole approach to theology and to Biblical studies. Even so, there is broad agreement on the methodology of scholarship: 'I am a conservative Christian, and I do my scholarly work on that basis. Another man is committed to a humanistic viewpoint and does his work on the basis of that. Neither of us is the better or the worse scholar, for the fact that we have different presuppositions. The question is whether we are prepared to acknowledge and examine and defend our presuppositions.' On methodological questions, Dick France is able to agree to a very large extent with most other people who are involved in mainstream New Testament scholarship. But the results will not necessarily be the same, because they may start from very different positions. 'Scholarship is more open now, in that we are more prepared to talk about these presuppositions. That is better than blackguarding one another with labels – radical, fundamentalist and so on. We do not use that sort of language so much now, and I'm glad of that. No one less than Bultmann himself argued years ago that exegesis without presuppositions was impossible. I agree with his conclusion, though not with all he said about what were the necessary presuppositions.'

Bultmann ruled out all possibility of miracles because he held that God cannot interfere with the closed causal framework of the world. We have seen that scientists are now less committed to such a closed set of mechanistic laws. There may be unique sets of conditions operating on occasion, and forms of personal interaction between the spiritual and the material world which are impossible to fit into the causal regularities of the natural sciences. After all, these only tell us what normally happens; they do not say that extraordinary things can never happen. There is no doubt, for instance, that Jesus is spoken of in the gospels as exorcising demons and healing all sorts of sickness. Must we regard these as complete legends; or is it possible to give some credence to them? The answer to this will again depend partly on one's wider views about whether psychical phenomena ever occur and have material effects. But of course in forming such wider views, the Biblical testimonies will be part of the evidence confirming the belief that such things as faith-healing take place. It will not be sufficient on its own; it will need corroboration from other sources. But it will be a significant part of the evidence for the primacy of spiritual causality in the universe.

It seems to me that on these matters it is hard to believe that all the accounts of healings and exorcisms we have, at many times and places in human history, are due to error or delusion. Bultmann's view seems to me very improbable, that the people of the New Testament had such a different world-view from us that we cannot possibly accept any of it; that there is someone called 'modern man' who knows that all these testimonies are incredible and even unintelligible to him. Dr France comments: 'Of course there is a massive cultural gap between us and the men of the Bible. That is where Biblical scholarship is necessary, to enable us as far as possible to bridge that gap and put ourselves in the shoes of those who wrote the Biblical books. There is then the very necessary process of translation of what they said within their context into appropriate forms of expression for our own situation. But it is also true that the cultural gap is nothing like as big as it is sometimes made out to be. What we think of as "modern man" is in fact only a very limited part of modern man. So, for instance, to believe in demons and witchcraft seems ludicrous from the western secular perspective; but when you have lived in Africa for a time you begin to realise that the world is a bit bigger than the western secular perspective makes it out to be.'

It is clear that Jesus was believed to have exorcised demons. Now if we believe there are no demons, this becomes very problematic for us. Dr France is prepared to believe that there are demons. An alternative possibility might be to say that Jesus worked within the context of beliefs operative in his culture, and was an effective exorcist in those terms. Just what the psychical or psychological realities underlying those beliefs are is very hard to say; but real healings were effected. We do not have to use those terms now, and for many of us it would not be possible to use them. But we might accept the testimony that Jesus really healed people described as demon-possessed, and was understood to be exorcising demons. The important point is that, working within the descriptions offered by his own culture, he made people whole and self-determining again. Professor Stanton, too, thinks that there is no reason why historians should be committed to total scepticism, in that the miracles in the gospels are no longer quite the difficulty that they have been in the past. We can accept that Jesus was a very remarkable person, with gifts of healing. The healing-miracles are not out of line with modern medical belief. We do now believe in the powers of faith as ways of healing. People do discover wholeness that includes physical healing as a result of religious faith. So he does not think there is any difficulty about those. And most of the miracles are of that order.

But not all of them are. In particular, the resurrection and the virgin birth are miracles of quite a different order, where God seems to mark off the beginning and end of a particular human life in a totally unique way. What are we to do with those accounts? Dick France comments: 'As far as the virgin birth is concerned, there are two questions. First, is the New Testament teaching that Jesus was born without a human father? And secondly, what do we do with that? On the first question, it seems to me there is absolutely no doubt whatsoever: that is what Matthew and Luke are saying. What we do with that is part of this whole question of world-views, and how we can take something that arose in one world-view and translate it into another. It seems to me that if you have problems recognising the possibility of a virgin birth, then you have problems recognising any other aspect of non-normal experience, of miracles. But if you have problems with the idea of a living, personal God who has particular purposes which he wants to bring about in the world, and who sometimes does things outside the normal course of events in order to bring them about, then a large part of the Christian faith is going to be meaningless.'

Dick France does not believe that the virgin birth is central to the whole theological structure of Christianity; but he does think that it is part of the revealed tradition. He thinks the historical probability of the early church developing a myth like this within a very short period of the life of Jesus, within the very context where the family of Jesus were themselves involved in the early growth of the church, very remote. 'People often suggest that the Christian church developed ideas out of pagan mythology. They often forget that the Christian church was a Jewish movement. It was not imbued with all the mythology of pagan Rome or Greece. What we have to talk about is what would have been possible within a pious Jewish context. In that context, the thought of a myth of virgin birth arising within a decade or two really is unthinkable.'

The virgin birth and the resurrection are so unexpected that most historians without any religious belief would have to discount their occurrence. But the whole point about them is that they are *supposed* to be unusual; they are supposed to be unique. They are supposed to mark off this human life of Jesus as of quite decisive importance in human history. In that sense, they are entirely natural, in the wider context of God's purpose; and, as we have noted, without the belief in the resurrection, the Christian faith would never have got started. So what can the historian do? He cannot take these accounts as *proving* that God acted in this way; but nor should he say that such a thing is impossible. He will simply have to record the belief; and then come to his own decision about what probably happened, on largely non-historical grounds. This recognition of the proper limits of the historical method has produced a greater degree of understanding between Biblical scholars of differing persuasions.

In the twenty-five years since Dick France was a student he has discerned a very noticeable change. 'As a student from a very conservative background, I felt myself constantly fighting against the enemy, battling against positions which I neither understood nor wanted to understand, and really having very little contact with people in other theological areas of thought. Nowadays I find that is not the case. I have good relationships with fellow New Testament scholars of all sorts of different theological positions. We listen to one another, talk with one another; the whole situation is a much more accepting and friendly and convergent situation – not that we agree on everything by a long way; but we agree to differ in a way which is much more positive than it used to be.'

It is a sign of the times that there is now a general acceptance of the usefulness of critical techniques to help understanding of what the Gospels really mean; so the orthodox no longer find themselves at such a great remove from the rest of the world. Still, conservatives do believe the Scripture is inspired. What does this mean? Does it raise an insuperable barrier between conservative and radical scholars? In answering the question, Dr France points out there are two senses in which 'inspired' may be used. 'I am not talking about it being inspired in the sense that one might say Bach is inspired, or the Beatles or whatever, in the sense that it is something that does something for me. I am talking more about its nature, its origin, the fact that it is not purely human.' If Christian theology is about revelation, about getting to know God, then it is reasonable to think there will be something which is not a purely human product, which is in some way disclosed by God himself, in order to give us the data we need. In the Bible, the authentic standard of revelation for Christians, one might expect to hear something other than just human voices. Of course, the human voices are there, and they are important. The Bible is obviously very human; it is written by real people in real situations, in ordinary human language, using their own cultural back-ground, thought-forms, historical experiences and so on. And it varies a great deal – one book of the Bible is very different from another, because of their different authors. But concurrent with this human origin, one may see the superintending work of God, ensuring that what is written will convey the truth he wants to convey. So, Dick France says, 'I would not talk about it as being just the Word of God or just the words of men; but rather the Word of God in the words of men.'

Inspiration, according to this view, is not some sort of divine dictation, with people passively writing down what God tells them. It is God's hidden over-seeing of the process, so that a true disclosure of his being and purpose is given in these documents. Whether you think this is a sensible presupposi-tion will depend on many factors – whether you think there could be a God who might wish to communicate his purpose to human beings, whether this purpose is morally and spiritually illuminating, and so on. I would judge that this *is* a sensible hypothesis, which must be tested by looking at the text in the light of it and seeing if it fits. Then the trouble is that many people point out inaccuracies and mistakes in the text; small things, usually, but enough to make you doubt whether it is all literally true. Dick France, though, does not necessarily see this as a problem for the conservative Christian: 'It is a rather dangerous assumption that you should take all the Bible literally. I hope that nobody would take all of Shakespeare literally. Why should one take all of the Bible literally either? Take it literally where it looks as if it is intended to be literal. But much of it is not; it is symbolic, poetic, it uses different forms of speech, as any other literature does. I would expect to interpret it according to what it seems to be intended to mean, the sort of literature it appears to be.' As with any literature, people may differ in their interpretation of it; and there will be room for people to disagree very radically about what the Bible is in fact saying. Dick France does not claim that he or anybody else has an infallible means of knowing what the Bible is intended to mean. It is, he says, simply a matter of trying to work at it and trying to be fair to the text.

There is an acceptance now, between scholars of many different persuasions, that there is room for plurality of interpretation; that much Biblical language is poetic and metaphorical; that the work of critical scholarship need not be destructive, but can open up new perspectives on the life of Jesus. The gulf between conservatives like Dick France and more radical thinkers in New Testament scholarship is not quite as great as it was. We have seen that there is general agreement on the main historical facts about Jesus. But it is essential to recognise that the Gospels were written in the light of a belief in the resurrection of Jesus. They give us a theologically interpreted history, trying to evoke in the reader the discernment of God the disciples had experienced. Faith expresses the meaning of Jesus' life, not the details of his biography. Facts are never going to compel a response of commitment in us; for such a response can only spring from a discernment of the love of God. While that will be a discernment of meaning in the facts, it can never be given just by the addition of more and more facts alone. Faith requires a different kind of response, and a different kind of vision. The techniques of history cannot evoke it.

Religious faith is not just a matter of possessing a lot of facts about historical happenings. If one person says to another, 'Have faith in me,' what is being said is, 'Trust me; follow me; take a risk by committing your life to me.' We don't need a vast amount of knowledge about Jesus to justify having faith in him. We do need enough information to give us reason to think that he is a reliable guide or spiritual teacher. But the best information we can have is really the testimony of others that he has renewed their lives. That is just what we have in the Gospels: the testimony of the early disciples that Jesus is worthy of our trust and loyalty. When they write about his life, they do not do so to give us exact biographical details. They are giving testimonies to evoke faith in us. Of course, these are based on remembered incidents and teachings; but they are written in order to bring out the meanings they discern in that life, to express their own discernment of God in Jesus. So they are very personal, and therefore very varied pictures; though they are indeed responses to a real historical person. That is the picture that recent New Testament scholars seek to put before us.

The voice of Biblical scholarship is not a destructive and negative voice. Perhaps it is true that earlier in this century some scholars saw the Gospels as largely fictional attempts at a biography; they thought we could know virtually nothing about the historical Jesus; they said that pure historical method would have to eliminate the miracles and healings; so that faith, if it still existed, would have to be divorced entirely from history. Such views have now been generally discredited. While not all Gospel scholars are Christians, it is entirely reasonable for one who commits his life to Christ, who believes that Christ is a living presence who makes God real to him, to interpret the records in the light of that resurrection-faith, to see them as expressions of the acts of God in history; for that is indeed how they were written. Christian faith cannot be divorced from history, because it is founded precisely on the claim that God reveals himself in history, and calls for a response to his action from those who discern it. But faith cannot be founded on history alone; just as love for another person cannot be founded simply on a biological study of their anatomy. Faith is a response of the total personality to the meaning which is revealed in the life, death and resurrection of Jesus. It is not just the intellectual belief that every sentence in the Bible is literally true.

That means there can never be complete agreement between Christian and non-Christian scholars about the historical basis of the Gospels. But we do not expect historians to agree, usually. What can be said is that there is enough agreement on the data to make the Christian response of faith a reasonable and appropriate one. The Gospel claims about Jesus are strong enough to pose an enormous problem to anyone seeking to understand Jesus in purely human terms, and reliable enough to evoke a rational response of faith and commitment. The critical wave has passed; and while it has left us valuable insights and forever changed our view of things, Biblical scholars in general now have a much more constructive, sympathetic and attractive story to tell of the person of Jesus and the origins of the Christian faith.

Chapter Six

OLD DOCTRINES IN A NEW WORLD

One of the best known theological remarks of recent years in Britain was the statement that David Jenkins, Bishop of Durham, made on a television programme: 'I wouldn't put it past God to arrange a virgin birth if he wanted but I very much doubt if he would.' At first sight, it seems unlikely that a bishop of the Church of England would have a greater insight into the mind of the Almighty than the writers of the Gospels, two of whom at least tell the story of the virgin birth. But part of what the bishop meant was that God does not perform gross physical miracles; he may influence people's minds, but he leaves their bodies strictly alone. On second thoughts, this is a bit odd, too; since it is very difficult to influence someone's mind without influencing important bits of their bodies, too – i.e. their brains. Whatever the pros and cons of it all, this episcopal pronouncement caused a sudden flurry of comment around the country. It must be said, however, that the comment was generally marked by its ignorance of most of what had been going on in Christian theology for the last hundred years; and it quickly became apparent that most people were quite unaware of the arguments that have been current in theology on these and allied subjects for some time now.

People got the virgin birth mixed up with the immaculate conception. They worried about whether bishops should be allowed to say what they think; and they speculated on whether God had sent down lightning on York Minster as a mark of disapproval. There was little comment on why the bishop should have said what he did; or on what Christian belief in the virgin birth really was or why it really mattered. Reactions tended to polarise into two camps, equally uncomprehending. One said: 'How shocking that the ancient truths of the faith should be attacked.' The other said: 'Thank goodness we do not have to believe those out-dated old myths any more.' Overall, I would judge that the general feeling was: 'Christians jolly well ought to believe in their old myths, even though they are quite false and not relevant to most of us at all.'

There is, however, a central theological issue at stake, which has been well discussed among theologians in recent years. It is the question of how God acts in the world – an enormously complicated and difficult problem, on the answer to which will depend one's interpretation of such things as the virgin birth and the resurrecion of Jesus. If we want to understand how God acts in the world, we must first, of course, have some idea of what we mean by 'God'; only then can we develop some idea of what a divine action might be. The orthodox Christian doctrine of God is, however, so little known that many people, even many Christians, are quite surprised when they hear it. I fear it must be said that there has been an almost complete failure of religious education in Britain. People who can be taught to do differential calculus and understand the structure of the atom have not been taught even the elementary moves in Christian theology; so theological arguments still have to be seen in terms of shock, horror and delicious scandal. And that, in a way, sums up the state of Christianity in Britain today. It is not that people know what it is, and have, generally speaking, rejected it. The fact is that few people have any idea of what Christianity actually is, or of the long and subtle history of reflection on Christian doctrines for thousands of years, in the East as well as in the western church. Things are so bad that some people can even be heard to say that Christianity is a western religion – this, despite the fact that it was born in the Middle East; and that the Orthodox churches of the East have preserved their tradition intact, apart from the Roman tradition of the Catholic Church, from which it has been divided since late antiquity. What most people in Britain are generally aware of is a very much simplified version of one of the Northern European or American versions of Protestantism, all hymn singing and hallelujahs, with little idea of what went on in Christian history more than one hundred years ago, when Moody and Sankey got going. They might read Billy Graham or John Stott; rarely do they get to Luther and Calvin; hardly ever to Aquinas; and Irenaeus and Athanasius may as well never have existed.

Why is this? How can religious education have been a compulsory subject in British schools since 1944, and such a vast ignorance exist? You often see advertisements in newspapers offering to tell you the great secret of the universe, locked up in the Great Pyramid or in some equally improbable place. But the biggest secret in Britain about Christianity is what its doctrines have actually taught, in their full depth and breadth. And one consequence of this is that we have lost a knowledge of the subtly stated and heavily qualified doctrines of the great theologians. We often have little sense of the way interpretations of doctrine have developed in different cultures and at different times, or of the primarily poetic and evocative character of the language of faith. The central Christian doctrines – about God, the incarnation, the Trinity and the atonement – are much more mysterious, much less straight-forward, than may appear at a superficial first sight. Indeed, these doctrines are called 'mysteries'; not problems or puzzles, but matters that cannot be said in literal or obvious ways without misunderstanding.

The first and most important thing in religion is to grasp the unsayability of its central topic, God. One contemporary British theologian who has tried to expound this tradition, to speak, paradoxically, of what cannot be spoken of, is John Macquarrie, who was Lady Margaret Professor of Divinity at Oxford until 1985, and perhaps the doyen of Anglican theologians: 'The idea of God is one of the most difficult that people can think about. One has got to explore it in such a way as to minimise the possibility of misunderstanding. Perhaps the chief misunder-standing has been to think of God in what I call monarchical terms, as if he were a kind of celestial emperor. Certainly that is not in accord with the Christian tradition, where stress is laid more on his love and his concern with his creation.'

For the monarchical idea, God is thought of chiefly in terms of sovereign power; he is the creator and ruler of the universe; he is the law-giver and often also the punisher of sins and deviations from his will. This does all tend to present a somewhat oppressive picture of God; and one can understand why many nineteenth-century atheists believed that if man is ever to be free, then he must abolish the idea of God. The problem is not that statements about God's power and ultimacy are false. It is that they can very easily be misinterpreted, to give the idea that God is a distant monarch who manipulates his creatures and acts in quite arbitrary ways with human beings, who are no more than his craven subjects. One source from which such a misinterpretation can arise is the Old Testament itself, which speaks of God as 'the sovereign Lord' with the power to do whatever he wills. Nevertheless, it would be a travesty of the Old Testament view of God to present it as a belief in an arbitrary manipulator of human affairs. God is thought of as a King, but also as a shepherd, bridegroom, as a storm god and a mountain god. What Professor Macquarrie calls the monarchical idea arises because these symbols are taken too literally, as though God was just like a man, writ large. But it is perfectly clear to any intelligent reader that these are poetic symbols. When the prophet Habakkuk writes of God, 'You rode upon the clouds; the storm cloud was your chariot . . . at the flash of your speeding arrows and the gleam of your shining spear the sun and the moon stood still . . . you trampled the sea with your horses and the mighty waters foamed' (Habakkuk 3,8-15), this is not a literal description of God. This armour-clad storm god, in his horse-drawn chariot, charging across the sky in fury, is a symbol for the judgement of God upon the evil of men.

And so it is with the other symbols of God in the Hebrew Bible. It is important to remember that the central dominating fact about the God of Israel is that he has no image. The Holy of Holies, at the heart of the most sacred spot in Jerusalem, the Temple, contains no visible representation of God. God cannot be literally represented in any way; and that is why it is forbidden to make graven images of God. If there is one main symbol for God in the Old Testament, it is the Shekinah, the cloud of glory whose dazzling light is too bright for any human being to penetrate. The Biblical testimony is really quite plain – that God in himself cannot be represented truly by human beings; and when the prophets speak in inspired symbolism, they are not saying God is really like that. They are saying: this is how we are to think of God, poetically. But we are to realise, at the same time, that God is far beyond anything we can imagine.

Thus men are to think of God as a King; but also to know that he is not like any earthly King, with the limitations, the greed and despotism, of any earthly King. Indeed, it should be plain that the God of Israel does not manipulate, but allows freedom, to sin or to do well. He responds to the acts of human beings, either judging their evil or blessing their penitence and righteousness. God is not a tyrant; he is responsive, patient and kind, even though he is a severe moral judge. Moreover, he is not arbitrary, acting only to cater for his own whims. He is moral and rational, acting to minimise evil and to help creatures realise all sorts of values. He delights in personal relationship with creatures, and shows constant love to his people. So, if we wish to be at all fair to the Biblical view of God, we must say that the Sovereign Lord is not an arbitrary tyrant. He is a moral and rational God who creates human beings to be free, and responds to their acts in judgement and in patient love. But we must remember, too, that God's nature is beyond our grasp; so all these symbols are really doing is to give us a way of thinking about God which will enable us to act appropriately towards him. In other words, the 'celestial emperor' view of God is wrong, only because earthly emperors are too evil and untrustworthy to be given unconditional obedience. For the Biblical view, the symbol of divine Kingship must be supplemented with the symbols of Fatherhood, of the Bridegroom delighting in his bride and, above all, of the Cloud of Glory which veils the divine reality.

It is this last symbol which has given rise to the main orthodox Jewish and Christian traditions of thinking about God. As Professor Macquarrie puts it: 'God is different from any finite or creaturely being. There must always be a sense in which he is incomprehensible; he is beyond the range of our human concepts. At best, we can have certain pictures, certain symbols, pointers in the right direction.' Virtually every major Jewish and Christian and Muslim thinker would agree with that. But many people probably still think that the orthodox view is that God is a person; omnipotent and all-knowing, perhaps, but still a person. That is not, strictly speaking, the case. 'God is more real than anything else. He is "Being-itself", the idea of being raised to a higher power, and our being is derivative from it. We think of God in personal terms, because of all the finite beings that we know, personal being seems to be the highest. Therefore it is the most appropriate to use in relation to God. Nevertheless, whatever finite image or analogy we may use, it still falls short of the reality of God, which must in itself go beyond the bounds of our understanding. So, while in liturgy and in prayer we use this personal language with respect to God, I don't think that exhausts the mystery of God's being. The word "supra-personal" makes sense to me; but this does not of course exclude that he has a personal dimension, to which we may relate.'

God is not, then, some sort of superman, hovering just above the clouds; he cannot even be literally described in any adequate way. God, for orthodox theologians, is the eternal and infinite source of reality which lies beneath all temporal and finite things. He is, as Macquarrie puts it, trying to render a thought of Thomas Aquinas in more recent philosophical terminology, 'Being-itself'. If this is so, then since all the main Christian doctrines are about God, they too will be indirect, poetic and not straightforwardly literal in meaning. That will naturally be true of all language about 'God acting', as well as of language which formulates the major Christian doctrines of the character of God and his relation to the world. It is certainly true of the doctrine of the Trinity, which has caused an enormous amount of misunderstanding and controversy.

The doctrine of the Trinity is not some sort of supernatural conjuring trick, whereby one being is equal to three beings. The best way to think of it may be to say that it presents three different symbols to enable us to understand the richness of God's being. Macquarrie says: 'The symbol of the Trinity reminds us that we can say of God that, on the one hand, he is a unity; there is only one God. But on the other hand, as the ultimate, he must contain in himself an unimaginable richness of being.' The use of more than one major symbol for God should help us to eradicate even more decisively that monarchical idea which some find so distressing. But why *three* symbols? That is due to the historical circumstances within which this disclosure of the nature of God occurred. At a very early stage in the development of the Christian church, the followers of Jesus found themselves beginning to use new language of God; beginning to say that God himself was present in the crucified and risen man Jesus; that in Jesus God himself had been expressed in a new way, and had acted in history in a new way to unite human beings to himself. Then they also found God as present within them, as the Holy Spirit, whom they described as labouring in travail in the creation to bring forth those goals which God intended to create.

Thus out of the experience of the early church, a new way of thinking about God began to emerge. And in time it developed into the fully-fledged fourth-century doctrine of the Trinity. According to this way of thinking, God is not just to be thought of as the creator, the origin, of all things, the Father or generator of all. He is also to be thought of as moving into the realm of finite beings and expressing himself there; entering into history to be with his creatures in a more intimate way. And this process is to be completed by the return of all things to God, to a fulfilment which is accomplished through the striving and creative action of the Spirit within the world. We might then say that all these three aspects together constitute God, in the way Christians have come to think of him as revealed to them through Christ.

We might think of it in this way: imagine a circle surrounded by a triangle. The circle is the Godhead itself, mysterious and unknowable, hidden in the cloud of glory. But this mystery is disclosed, through the life of Jesus, in the three-pointed symbol of the Father, who always remains the creative personal source of the universe; the Son, expressing the eternal reality of God in time; and the Spirit, taking all temporal things back into unity with God, and so fulfilling the temporal in the eternity from which it came. If we can think of it in terms rather like that, we might see that Christians believe in the same one God as Jews and Muslims. But the distinctive contribution made by Christian belief to the general idea of God is that God expresses himself in history. When we talk of God's action, we are most fundamentally speaking of God's temporal self-manifestation in the universe. And we are speaking of the particular ways in which this takes place in one specific part of space and time, in the history of this planet.

When Christians talk about Jesus being the 'Son of God', then, they are not to be taken literally – as if God was really a genetically male member of the human species, who passes on his deoxyribonucleic acid to Jesus. Once clearly stated, that view is absurd, and has never been held by any major Christian theologian. A much more subtle account must be offered of how a particular man can express the mystery of God. Rowan Williams, Professor Macquarrie's successor at Oxford, considers that the reason many people say it is no longer possible to believe in the incarnation is that they do not have a very clear idea of what that doctrine was meant to be saying. 'You could read some attacks on this doctrine in recent years and come away with the impression that for twenty-odd centuries Christians had believed that somehow or other God turned himself into something he was not. That creates some kind of logical contradiction. How can a man be a man and a rabbit at the same time? How can a man be a man and a God at the same time? I'm sure that is not what the great Christian theologians were trying to say. As I read the evidence in the early church, and indeed in the medieval church when the doctrine was developed far more than many people realise, the picture I get is quite simply this: here is a human being, Jesus of Nazareth, who is in every respect an ordinary human being. He has a body, he has a mind, he has emotions and he stands in a unique relationship with God, a relationship so unique that nobody else has a relationship like it. His entire life is somehow an expression and articulation in our world of God. There is no corner of Jesus' life that is not pervaded by the life of God. At the same time, that does not alter the fact that he is a human being. According to the classical theologians of the church, what changes in the incarnation is not God. God does not come down from heaven to earth in an absolutely literal sense. But a human being comes into existence who is absolutely and perfectly in harmony with God, who reflects and expresses the life of God as Son. That may not be easy to believe, but at least it is not manifestly logically contradictory; and not nearly as silly as some people try to make it sound.'

Some feel rather uneasy with this language, as if it is somehow reducing the traditional faith; so it is important to emphasise that Professor Williams takes himself to be representing the views of the orthodox theologians, in a way more appropriate to our own age. He does not use the concept of 'identity', saying bluntly that Jesus is identical with God. But that is because that concept has demonstrably misled people into thinking that Jesus must have been omnipotent and omniscient, or that God must have given up the government of the universe, leaving nobody in charge while he was on earth. Instead, he uses words like 'expresses', 'reflects' and 'articulates', to try to explain how a finite human person can represent in time the nature of a God who is infinite and beyond time and personhood, as we understand it. He is emphatically not saying that the man Jesus later becomes God, because of his perfection or sinlessness. Jesus, for Christians, was God from the very first moment of his life, by the initiative of God himself assuming a human nature to himself. But it is an enormously difficult philosophical task to say how it is that a human life can be the visible and appropriate image for God, who is strictly speaking beyond both images and imagination. To work it out at all requires enormous sophistication and subtlety – which the church fathers have indeed given it, in the philosophical terms available in their own epochs. The important point is that, once one grasps the mystery of God, one can see that the incarnation is meant to be the expression in time of that mystery. It is quite unfair, therefore, to dismiss it as some of the contributors to John Hick's volume, *The Myth of God Incarnate*, did. The doctrine is not just a piece of imaginative invention. It is a serious and sustained attempt to comprehend how the mystery of God had been disclosed to the disciples in the person of Jesus.

The idea of incarnation is not confined to Christianity; parallels can be found in other religions. With Vishnaism in India, for example, there is the notion of God's descent, God's coming among human beings in human form and sharing in human life. But these avatars, as they are called, like Krishna, are not fully human beings; they are more appearances of the gods in human form. Nor do they fit into the prophetic tradition, and so fulfil a particular historical expectation and role as Jesus did. They also lack any idea of the suffering and death of a saviour god, which has become such a central part of the Christian faith. Nevertheless, these doctrines are ways of saying that God cares about our human concerns and that he in some way shares in them in order to lead humankind to himself. They are ways of expressing the belief that the eternal God expresses himself in time; and that in some particular parts of the temporal process his own nature may be directly manifested.

If the doctrine of the incarnation is a doctrine about how the eternal God can be expressed in time, in a way suited to human understanding, it should be clear that one can believe in the doctrine of the incarnation without believing in the doctrine of the virgin birth. Indeed, if you just think that Jesus was a man who had no human father, a biological freak, and do not realise what the incarnation is really about, you have missed the whole point. That is what David Jenkins is very much concerned to say. At the same time, if Jesus was miraculously born, that does have a theological point of its own to make. It shows that Jesus was not just a man who was later raised to great status by God. His human nature was, from the very first moment of its existence, united in a uniquely close way to God, so that Jesus always had a clear and vivid knowledge of the divine being and was in a pre-eminent way the channel of the creative acts of the divine spirit. The importance of this is that it shows that God took the initiative, to unite human nature to himself; and it shows that we can be united to God, too, by our relationship to Christ. It shows these things, not in some abstract theological discourse, but in a way the simplest person can grasp – by stating that Jesus was born simply by the decree of God, without a human father. As he was unique in his death and resurrection, so he was unique in his beginning. And though at first only his immediate family, perhaps only Mary and Joseph, would have known this, it became a memory treasured in the early church, which helped to mark him out from all other human beings as unique.

The virgin birth is not in itself important. It can even be misleading, if it leads one to think that sex is sinful or that Jesus was not really a man – both heretical beliefs, in the eyes of orthodoxy. Yet it does seem a fitting and appropriate symbol of God's action in entering into time and uniting human nature to himself, at a particular point in history when such an action could be most effective. Some theologians would say it was only that – a symbol which was later put into historical form, though it never really happened. I think that is what the Bishop of Durham would say. We must be clear that a great many theologians would say that – including many Roman Catholic theologians, too. After all, it might well be said of many Old Testament miracles, like God leading the Israelites through the wilderness in a pillar of cloud and fire, that they did not literally happen. What has happened is that poetic forms of describing God's leadership of his people have got turned into factual accounts, some time after the event. It is as if poetry has been turned into prose. If you then say that these events did not happen, that may be said to be irrelevant to the main point, which all the time lay in the poetic expression of an inner relation to God. Thus it is not outrageous to give a similar sort of account to the virgin birth, and to the resurrection too, interpreted as a bodily raising from the tomb.

The question that needs to be asked is how important actual historical occurrences are to these accounts; and how far they are adequately interpreted as outward symbols for inner spiritual experiences. We have noted that all our talk about God must be in some sense symbolic; certainly talk about God 'entering time' and 'uniting humanity to himself' is highly metaphorical. That does not mean it is false. But it does mean that its truth is peculiarly opaque and not adequately conceivable by us. Nevertheless, it is a central part of the Christian tradition that God is thought of as acting, as taking the initiative to bring about some state of affairs for a purpose. So, in the Old Testament, God is spoken of as calling Israel to follow him, as leading them out of Egypt, as punishing them for sin and promising them his blessing in future. Even if we would be wrong to think of God literally as a person who keeps interfering in the lives of these people from time to time; yet we must think of their history, at the very least, as woven into a larger purposive design, a moral and purposive process. They are continually called to respond to events which demand of them a specific discernment of the divine purpose and a commitment to it. In the New Testament, the divine initiative takes the form of shaping a particular human life so that it becomes a perfected expression of the Divine nature; and that through Jesus' death and resurrection a new community, empowered by the Holy Spirit, is born.

These initiatives and these purposes must be historical. They cannot be purely inward, with no outer, material effects. It does, no doubt, need a special sort of discernment to see the hand of God in them; but it must make a real difference to the world that God has specific purposes for it. Stephen Sykes, the Regius Professor of Divinity in the University of Cambridge, states: 'I would say that the Christian faith is committed to the defence of the view that God acts in human history. I do not see how you can have a notion of Divine action which does not entail believing that there are effects in human history which can be identified as being what they are because of a divine initiative.'

The only question, then, is what sort of effects those are. The answer to that must surely be that we cannot work it out just by thinking about it. We have to look and see what discernments of the divine purpose are claimed to have occurred. The remarkable fact is that the only basic religious tradition which has consistently claimed that there is a divine purpose, a moral goal, for this world, is the prophetic tradition of ancient Israel. The goal, as it came to be conceived in the late prophetic tradition, is the establishment of the Kingdom of God, a just society on earth. To bring about this goal, God chooses a particular people and calls them to be a Kingdom of priests, set apart to keep his Law. For Christians, Jesus is the fulfilment of the prophetic dreams of Israel, who opens up the Kingdom to the whole world by the gift of the Spirit. So God is seen as acting in very particular ways; and this raises a problem for many. Why should God choose the Jews? Or the Christians? Is it really conceivable that a loving God should give salvation only to those who follow Moses or Jesus? How can God be so arbitrary?

'If it is reasonable to believe that this world is God's world, we do not have to hold that he always operates towards it in the same kind of way,' says Colin Gunton, Professor of Christian Doctrine at King's College, London. 'If you ask, why does God act in particular ways in history, rather than operating according to one regular pattern, I think you have to say it is because he is a personal God. If he operated in exactly the same way all the time, that would almost be like saying that he does not really make any difference to our world at all. In the Bible, we get a picture of a God who, while caring for the world overall, yet makes himself present in different ways to his people. The incarnation is the completion of part of the history of God with Israel, expanding it into all the world and for all human beings, however this will work itself out in the end.'

It is indeed characteristic of persons that they do not always do the same things on all occasions. They react appropriately – if they are wise – to different circumstances. According to the Biblical record, God took one particular group of people; and through a succession of prophetic leaders a tradition was built up which prepared the way for the coming of the Kingdom. It is perhaps a pointless question to ask why that did not happen elsewhere, since it was what God chose to do. But, from a Christian point of view, it is impossible to think of Jesus except as the Messiah, the culmination of a long process of hope and expectation in Judaism. He could not just have appeared anywhere; the preparation for his life was long and continuous, over many years. Professor Gunton comments: 'A number of theologians have taught that the incarnation is the centre of God's activity towards his world. There is a sense in which it belongs in the eternal love of God, to make himself one with his creatures in this particular way.' That is, the formless God who is beyond all human thought has always willed to make himself known in personal form, in a human life which expresses in a way we can receive and respond to, the mystery of the Divine nature. The second-century Christian theologian Irenaeus put the point in a very pregnant way when he said, 'The glory of God is a man fully alive.'

We might say, then, that it was always God's purpose to express his being in human form. But why should he do it just once, in Jesus of Nazareth? Colin Gunton again: 'If we understand the world as a reality open to the action of God, we will think that in some way God is always upholding and operating within the world. The incarnation is the central moment in one continuous process by which God brings human life to its proper completion.' The incarnation is not a wholly discontinuous event, interrupting an otherwise purely human story. The world is always open to the actions of God. And the great purpose that God is working out in the world is the salvation of creation – its being brought to wholeness and completion. So Christians speak of the events surrounding Jesus not only as the 'incarnation' of God in time, but also as the 'atonement', the making-one, of God and humanity.

Naturally, the God who is Love wills all human beings to be united to him. But humans are beings with a history, with life-stories to tell, which build up into patterns of distinctive meaning and significance. The uniting of God and humanity cannot be accomplished by a sudden discontinuous intervention into history; at least not if human freedom and the distinctive character of the human search for meaning is to be preserved. It is accomplished by a progressive series of particular acts which successively broaden out to include the whole planet. Thus we can see the incarnation prepared for by a long prophetic tradition, shaping that particular Jewish culture within which alone Jesus could be understood as the Son of God. And we can see the church as born at a time in history when it could quickly spread throughout the decaying Roman Empire. The story is by no means finished yet; and we cannot tell how new influences and interactions may yet modify it, before that day when Christ comes in glory – that is to say, when God's own self-expression in time is seen in clear and full manifestation, and the long process of atonement is at last completed.

The atonement has sometimes been spoken of as though God required the sacrifice of some innocent human being to save people from eternal punishment. Widespread though such a view seems to be, it is in fact a crude version of an eleventh-century theory – that of Anselm. It can make no claim to be the standard Biblical view. A fuller study of the early Christian theologians shows it to be a misrepresentation of just one metaphor for atonement among many in the New Testament. It is true that Christ died; but, on the orthodox Christian view, this is an expression of the self-giving of God himself so that humans might be forgiven and freed from their guilt and evil, their ignorance and despair. The cross is a central Christian symbol for the being of God himself. We cannot say that God literally suffers on the cross; that would not make sense, given the orthodox doctrine of God as beyond literal description. But nor should we say that the crucifixion of Jesus is just the death of a man with whom God sympathises. The cross is a Mystery, in the fullest sense – that is, not just something we cannot explain; but a true expression in time of the ineffable God, which expresses for us what God is and does. In that sense, it is the central act of God in human history.

For Christians the atonement is not just a showing of what God is; it is an action of God in the further sense that it forgives human sin – it removes from us all that stands between us and God himself. In that way, it does save us from eternal death; that is, from final separation from God. It mediates to us eternal life, life in relation to the eternal. And it does this as we incorporate it into our own lives, becoming sharers in the death of Christ that we may be made one with God.

If these are the images which mediate God to us, which make us one with God, they have had to be built up in a very complex way through a cumulative tradition of human responses to discernments of God in history. As I shall suggest more fully in chapter seven, this does not exclude all other human beings from salvation. But it does mean that the definitive form of salvation, the wholly adequate expression of God, the appropriate way to relate to him and the authentic means of relating to him, is progressively given in the long tradition which leads from Abraham to Jesus and beyond. It is not that God appeared just once, long ago on the shores of an insignificant lake, and then disappeared for ever. Rather, the long-term purpose of the uniting of humanity to God is being progressively worked out throughout the whole earth. But at the centre of that process, Christians claim, is the figure of a man who, because of the unique nature of the culture in which he was born, the unique set of expectations prepared for his coming and the unique character of his own relation to God, has become the one through whom God reconciles the world to himself, the Christ.

If this is the sort of way in which contemporary British theologians see the great doctrines of the Trinity, the incarnation and the atonement, then it seems that at the present time there is a great rethinking of doctrine going on which is not a simple return to the past, but a creative refashioning of ancient traditions in the light of new perceptions. One of the problems with these doctrines is that they have been given an over-literal interpretation, and the sense of religious symbolism, of mystery and of the evocative character of religious language has been lost. It was a former Bishop of Durham, Ian Ramsey, who did much to restore a sense of the elusiveness and poetic nature of religious language, though his work is not yet as widely known as it should be among Christians.

What happens when over-literal interpretations are given is that the Trinity comes to be thought of as an everlasting committee meeting – a man, a boy and a mysterious bird, locked for ever in mutual flattery. The incarnation then becomes a matter of one of these three persons trying to get inside the head of a human being, or even take over a human personality like some mad scientist, and make it perform a number of magical tricks before finally shooting off into space like a prototype rocket. And the atonement is a savage god requiring the death of an innocent human being, so that he can let everyone else off their due punishments with honour satisfied. These are caricatures; but I suspect that the ideas some people have about Christian doctrines are uncomfortably close at times.

The way to root out these misconceptions is really to go back and re-examine the traditional teachings of the orthodox theologians; not to throw out the doctrines themselves, as some more radical thinkers have suggested. Stephen Sykes says: 'The traditions of the past, which have been developed with very great subtlety and skill, deserve an extremely long and careful hearing, in the contemporary church – a longer and more careful one than they actually get at the hands of some modern theologians. We must look very carefully at the plausibility of the supposed new constructions before rushing to embrace them. There is a sort of impatience with the past which is not entirely constructive and helpful as a feature of the contemporary theological scene. Some modern theologians who are very impatient with these things summarise and dismiss them in a couple of sentences; but because they have not given a careful account in the first place, the reader wrongly thinks that he is in the presence of some great original genius. I think it helps, when dealing with doctrinal problems, if you have a clear understanding of the history of the Christian tradition, as well as a knowledge of the problems of modernity.'

The suggestion is not that one should simply restate the doctrines of the ancient world, but that one should make a sympathetic effort to grapple with problems that have long been recognised, even if in different terms and languages. To throw the tradition out is cultural barbarism; to repeat it thoughtlessly is blind authoritarianism; but to recover its concerns and understand it properly is to grow in understanding of what the Christian faith means, in its full depth and subtlety. I have suggested that, if one does that, it becomes at once apparent that the orthodox doctrine of God requires a rejection of straightforwardly descriptive language about God and his actions. So, in talking about the Trinity, one is talking about the symbols for ultimate reality which have grown out of the Christian experience. In speaking of the incarnation, one is speaking of how the eternal has been disclosed in time. And in speaking of atonement, one is trying to come to grips with the way in which human lives can be brought to fulfilment by response to those discernments of meaning which have come to us through Jesus.

Thus it is central to Christian faith to say that one commits one's life in response to disclosures of God which come to one in historical events, perhaps through other people or through the circumstances one finds oneself in. Moreover, God shapes certain events so that they will truly be disclosures of his own being; they become intentional expressions of God, or acts of God. The Christian faith did not start as a set of difficult doctrines. It started with a response to an actual life, the story of a man. Stephen Sykes: 'The story of Jesus is appropriately regarded as the raw material of Christian doctrine. Story is the sort of thing that means that the faith can be communicated to everybody. You do not have to be a theologian at all, to understand what the Christian faith is about. But at the same time, for virtually the entire history of Christianity, there has been a terrific intellectual endeavour to attempt to interpret responsibly what the implications of this story are, and what the objections are to which it is open.'

The great Christian doctrines, like that of the Trinity, arise out of attempts to understand the story of Jesus in the light of a general belief in a moral and providential God. But the story itself is primary; it enshrines the basic disclosures of the acts of God in the life of a human being. If you ask, 'Can this story be historically authenticated?', the answer must be 'no', if by that you mean could it be established beyond doubt that it happened just as recorded. But that is hardly the point. For the religious question about the story is, 'What is disclosed of God here?', and 'What am I summoned to do, in response to this disclosure?' The Gospels provide for us a record of the disclosures of God which for the first Christians came through Jesus. It is not possible for us to disentangle what really happened from what has been written to express a theological reflection on the story. And if that is not possible, there is little point in trying. We must confine ourselves to the story as we have it, and say, 'What we have here is a testimony to the discernment of God in the life of a man.'

In such a situation, it is surely right to expect and accept a measure of pluralism about the exact interpretations we might offer of such things as the virgin birth and the resurrection, viewed as objective, bodily occurrences. Our interpretations will be merely speculative enterprises, in any case; whereas what matters, religiously, is what you discern of God in those stories and how that discernment transforms your life in practice. Thus Rowan Williams says: 'There is an enormous amount of disagreement about the resurrection among theologians. There are some who say that all we really need is that the awareness of the apostles changed dramatically after the death of God – so dramatically that you can say it is a kind of miracle. It was God giving them hope and trust back again after the cross; and that is really all we need to say. But there are other people, and I am one of them, who do not think that God only works inside people's heads. The way we actually come to know things is by seeing real events in the world. We do not just learn by mysterious little private events in our consciousness. That is why to learn what the resurrection speaks of, to learn that God is still with us, that God forgives us even beyond our furthest abandonment of him – to learn all that, we need something rather more concrete than just a new set of ideas, even if they are implanted by God miraculously in our heads. And I must say that if God can miraculously implant ideas in people's heads I do not quite see why he cannot miraculously disimplant Jesus from his grave.'

We might say that the outer limit of Christian belief about the resurrection is that the nature of God is truly discerned in the story of the cross, and that we can now realise the spiritual presence of Christ within us as we respond to it. Professor Williams argues that God acts in a more outward, objective way than that; he really does transfigure the body of Jesus into a new and glorious form, no longer limited by physical laws. And in this body he appeared to the apostles. It is important to realise that both these views can well come down to the same thing, in personal experience, where what counts is personal commitment to a disclosure of God as finding victory through suffering, of love being undefeated in death. But it is true that a physical transfiguration would be, in a sense, a more compelling and unambiguous sign of Divine action. Rowan Williams does not, however, feel the same way about the virgin birth, where he inclines to think that the testimony is not strong enough for commitment to this as an actual physical event. As I noted in chapter five, scholars like Dick France would retort that the testimony is there, and that is that. Perhaps we can say that the dispute is not about whether God acts, but about how publicly and physically he acts, in ways contrary to the usual regularities of nature.

Like the disputes about the reliability of Scripture, these disputes about the nature of divine action seem irresolvable by their very nature. Does that mean that the whole fabric of Christian doctrine is beginning to fall apart in a very public way? Professor Sykes thinks not: 'Conflict has always accompanied Christianity, right from the very earliest days. The medieval period was one in which there was very vigorous debate between theologians of different persuasions. It is the normal state for Christianity, and a very healthy one too. Unfortunately, the Christian church developed quite severe modes of repressing certain sorts of argument in the past. That kind of repression has always been counter-productive. It just does not work to try and end an intellectual argument by silencing one or other of the parties. The last two hundred years has shown that it is enormously difficult to draw the precise boundaries of acceptable belief. That does not mean that they do not exist; but I see no reason to think that we have to be absolutely clear on where the boundary is.'

It seems that in modern British theology there is both a return to tradition, as a source for the restatement of the great central doctrines of incarnation and atonement, and an acceptance of a greater pluralism of interpretation about the nature of God's action in the world. Strange as it may seem at first, these two things go naturally together. For the dogmas of the church were not framed to be definitive philosophical categories, preventing all further thought; they are the guardians of mystery and the many-sidedness of faith. As Rowan Williams says: 'I think it is certainly possible to hold traditional Christian doctrines in an intelligent, intelligible and critical way. All doctrinal language aims not to sum up and to deal exhaustively with how God works with us; far from it. When we speak of God and his work in Christ, there must always be a very profound sense of the inadequacy of what we say, a necessary reticence. We must not ever suppose that it is easy to talk about God, about Trinity and incarnation. But these are the words which are hammered out of centuries of complex, difficult Christian experience. These are the words which carried that experience and the hopes that went with it, which have served many people since their first formation, as carriers of their hopes and experience. We are not supposing that we can describe the domestic life of God, or what it felt like to be Jesus of Nazareth. That would be ridiculous. We are saying, only words of this scale and this scope can do justice to that extraordinary changing of our horizons, the remaking of our mental and imaginative world that happens in faith.'

What can now be seen is that the formulae of faith are symbolic and poetic; that the faith needs continually to be re-interpreted in the light of constantly changing knowledge; that a questioning faith and an admission of a good deal of ignorance about God's ways are not new weaknesses, but ancient strengths. A greater understanding of the Christian tradition will reveal a deep agnosticism at its core, an agnosticism rooted in the positive insight that the mystery of God is beyond human comprehension. This is coupled with a reverent devotion to Christ, as the one whose story, re-presented in the community of the church, is the present summons of God to us to pursue human fulfilment both in society and in our own lives. This is in a way a return to a more conservative view;

but not in a superficial way. For the true conservatism of faith does not lie in the traditions of a century ago; but in a recovery of the insights of the great saints and spiritual teachers. Their testimony is that of the angelic doctor, Thomas Aquinas, who began his greatest work by saying, 'We do not know what God is, but only what he is not'; and who, after a life of theological writing, said, 'All I have written is as straw.'

Christian doctrines are not just odd beliefs about improbable historical happenings. Their function is to enshrine potent symbols for setting human lives in the perspective of eternity. These symbols were born in the life of a community, as it responded to what it discerned of God in Jesus. For some, these will remain symbols which do not presuppose or entail miraculous occurrences, in a historical sense. For others, miracles will seem to be natural and intelligible transformations of the temporal process by inclusion in the divine purpose. For both, the central question of faith must be: does God speak through the life and words of Christ, as they are preserved for us by the early church? Do we discern in him an icon of eternity? And does God bring us to inner fulfilment, the joy which lies in the knowledge and love of the eternal Self, as we respond to that discernment? The story exists to evoke the faith in us which transformed the life of the early church. The doctrines exist to draw out its wider implications, in the light of our other well-established knowledge of the world in which we live.

This, I think, represents the way in which Christian doctrines are seen by most contemporary British theologians. Of course, arguments will continue about miracles and about the precise interpretation of the doctrines. But there is an increasing readiness to re-examine and rethink the ancient traditions of faith; a refusal to over-simplify so as to fit all doctrines into one neat, precisely formulated package; and a determination to preserve intellectual and moral integrity in faith. The old doctrines can live again in a new world; because their primary intent was always to present ways of opening human vision to the presence of eternity; and the revelations of God are the ways in which that eternity makes itself known to us.

It is clearly difficult to communicate this understanding of Christian doctrine; the urge to over-simplify and caricature is strong in all of us. But it is arguable that the devastating self-criticism which has characterised recent Christianity may prove the foundation of an enduring strength. Christian theology, as I have tried to show very briefly in this chapter, is in a lively and confident mood. It expresses a renewal of concern for the recovery of a spiritual dimension in human life, and a renewed appreciation of the spiritual wealth of two thousand years of Christian tradition. It is a rigorous and demanding discipline; but it promises to uncover depths of understanding human life, ignorance of which would be an impoverishment of spirit, and an irreparable loss to British culture.

Nevertheless, Christianity is by no means the only religion in Britain. Though it is important to understand the past, one must also look positively to the future; and in this respect Christians in Britain have to accept that they will be only one religious faith among others, even if the largest. So, while Christian theologians may have a confident sense of the importance of their own tradition and its spiritual and moral resources, it would by myopic in the extreme to ignore the traditions of others. In considering the state of Christianity in Britain, therefore, it is necessary to examine the other faiths which exist; to ask what they have to say to the Christian tradition, and how Christians should seek to relate to them.

Chapter Seven

GODS MANY AND LORDS MANY

In the classical Indian tradition, there are 33 gods. However, gods have an almost irresistible tendency to multiply themselves, sometimes in the most peculiar ways. And before very long the Hindus were able to record that there were 33 million gods and goddesses. That may be a pardonable exaggeration; but there may well be 33 million religions. As you look around in Britain, a good may of them seem to be alive and well. In the first chapter, I pointed out that there were perhaps more Muslims than Baptists in Britain. But there are also Hindus, Buddhists, Jews, Rastafarians – as well as many fairly new cults like Scientology, Rajneeshism, Soka Gokkai and so on. Today there exists something rather like a religious supermarket – you can look around the shelves and choose what most appeals to you. Christianity is just one of the many sects and faiths on offer, and not always the obvious choice.

The change to a religiously plural society has been rapid and dramatic; so much so that people can feel disorientated, and the existence of so many faiths within one society has become a problem. To some it is a threat to traditional British culture. To some it just makes the whole business of religion so complex that they give up. To others it poses an exciting new opportunity, though they are sometimes not quite sure what for. How do Christians in Britain cope with this new situation?

I think the major response – which matches the mood of penitence about our imperial past – is to repent of having sent out lots of missionaries to make tribal people dress in trousers and skirts, and to set about retracting the old exclusivist Christian claim, that only Christianity is true, and all else is totally false or without value for salvation. It is obvious, on even cursory examination, that members of other faiths than Christianity pray and achieve a high level of moral and spiritual life; that they find both comfort and challenge in their faiths; and that they can be very sophisticated, and not at all like primitive savages bowing down to gods of wood and stone. There has been a shock to the effortless superiority of Christianity.

Now of course there shouldn't have been such a shock. The diversity of faiths is not new, and Christianity was born and grew in cultures where many religions already flourished. In the early days especially, Christianity interacted with many faiths, incorporating much of them into itself, and developing rapidly by a sort of oscillating process of assimilation and rejection. The great festivals of Christmas and Easter have taken over old religious elements; Easter eggs and Christmas trees have nothing especially Christian about them, and even the Buddha has got into the Christian act, under the name of St Jehoshaphat. There have been many interactions between religions. Nevertheless, it is just silly to say that all religions are the same when Christianity has been so antagonistic to Judaism and Islam, especially, throughout its turbulent history, and when even Plymouth Brethren and Roman Catholics find it hard to agree on any two things. Christianity is a set of traditions which has always existed alongside other religions, stressing its own distinctive emphases and making its own accommodations to the culture it happens to be in.

What seems to have happened in Britain – and a similar sort of thing happens everywhere from time to time – is that the Christian faith has got identified in the public mind with a certain kind of Northern European Protestantism, modified by a sort of down-to-earth pragmatism which enables us to sort out the practically useful from the 'merely theological', without too much intellectual fuss. Into this atmosphere exotic new religions have poured, disturbing the reliance on tradition and that tacit commitment which has marked so much of British life. Now we are daily asked to choose between a whole host of strange varieties, and we haven't any idea of how to go about doing it. The consequence has been that Christians have been forced to ask just what is distinctive about their faith, and how far it is inextricably bound up with a particular form of culture. And this, in turn, has led many of them to realise that what they really valued or lived with wasn't very much like a distinctive form of Christianity at all. It was what is often called now 'folk religion' – a way of relating to whatever sacred or supernatural forces there may be, through whatever rituals and symbols are given by the religious institutions nearest to hand.

This can be seen quite clearly when keen young clergymen visit parents whose children are about to be baptised. They try, in their zeal, to get the parents to become 'real' Christians; and this comes as a shock, and often as an affront to the hapless parents, who, in the first place, thought they were real Christians, and are offended to be challenged. But, in the second place, when they find out what the clergyman thinks real Christians are, they want nothing to do with it. The confrontation is between the articulate, though often humanly insensitive priest, and the theologically inarticulate but stubbornly tacit Christian; and that can be a recipe for disaster.

This is one reaction of the churches to the new religions – retreat into a defensive theological castle. The trouble is, it makes religion much too intellectual; divorced from its roots in culture, or – even worse – associated with a defence of traditional culture against new tendencies in society. A new and arid intellectualism grips many of the churches, excluding those who cannot, or do not wish to, see faith in such clear-cut and literate terms. So the church becomes a sect and retreats to the margins of social life – an option for those who are interested, but not being, and not wishing to be, integrated into the culture itself.

At a more reflective level, the response is different. For though there have always been many religions, these religions change and develop, largely by interaction with one another, whether acknowledged or not. So the Hinduism we now see in Britain is quite different from that which existed in India a thousand years ago. Modern Hinduism has a new international face. It has been effectively transformed by men like Radhakrishnan, President of India from 1962 to 1967, and a profound religious thinker; and Krishnamurti, who presented Hinduism, not as the ethnic faith of the Indians, bound for ever to the caste system, but as an international faith which was all-embracing and all-inclusive. It is this profoundly westernised system which one meets, at least at the level of thinking and writing, in Britain. So the meeting between Christian and Hindu today in Britain is quite different from any meeting which could have taken place between followers of Jesus and of the Veda two thousand years ago. The influences which have shaped both of them in the meanwhile make any meeting now a new and complex one.

One of the theologians who has been most influenced by such a meeting is John Hick, who was Professor of Theology at Birmingham University, and is now at the Claremont Graduate School in California. He was especially impressed by the Sikh community in Birmingham, and has incorporated much of their thinking into his own work. The change it has brought about in his thinking can be clearly seen in the fact that one of his books had two titles. When it first came out, he called it, *Christianity at the Centre*, but the second edition was retitled *The Centre of Christianity*. What had happened in the meanwhile was that he no longer saw Christianity as the centre of world religions, with the others grouped around the periphery. Rather, Christianity stood with the others on that periphery; and only God, a mysterious God known by a thousand names, stood at the centre. Hick was convinced by the faith and love of the Sikhs he knew that Christianity and Sikhism were both valid ways to God, different paths to come to know the transcendent. So he can remain in the Christian tradition without any longer making any claims to exclusiveness or even to superiority. It is his way to God, but not the only way, and not the best way for everyone.

This is a response which attracts many who think that Christianity cannot be the only way to salvation, and that it cannot claim a monopoly of truth. But it does have its problems. It surely cannot be true that every religion is an equally valid way to a totally mysterious god, even the cranky and spurious ones. There simply has to be some process of selection. Otherwise I could start a religion tomorrow, called Beebism, and claim that its worship, which consists of watching BBC 1 every night, is a perfectly valid way to God; and that wouldn't sound very convincing (I hope). So we simply have to start sorting out the respectable from the non-respectable religions, whether we like it or not.

John Hick's own criterion seems to be that any religious system which has lasted a long time, and satisfied many wise and good people, must have something in it. Fifty thousand Frenchmen can't be wrong. But of course you still can't avoid deciding which people are good and wise. For I wouldn't like to be committed to the view that whatever most people believe most of the time is true – that seems to be a recipe for blind prejudice and unthinking traditionalism. No, we begin assessing a religion by looking at the moral stature, the intellectual acumen, the imaginative insight and the sensitivity of at least some of its adherents. That still won't show you that a religion is true; but it will show that it is to be taken seriously.

The real trouble is that various religions spend a lot of their time saying just what is wrong with their competitors. Within Hinduism, Ramanuja says that Sankara is deluded and ignorant; while the Buddha is reported to have said that the whole Vedantic tradition which those two share is mere stupidity and foolishness. The Muslims are quite clear that the Koran has spoken the final word, and that the doctrine of the Trinity comes very near to idolatry, and is certainly mistaken. And Christians have usually rejected the whole tradition of rebirth and the eternal repetition of the universe which underlies most of Indian thought. Even when someone starts a religion which tries to reconcile previous faiths he usually ends up by having yet another faith which insists that all the others are wrong. Thus the Sikh religion, formed as a way of reconciling Muslim and Hindu ideas, has ended by having to say that all traditional Muslims and Hindus are mistaken. It looks as if religion breeds infinite differences, and there is little prospect for agreement at all. When a scholar like Cantwell Smith writes a book called *Towards a World Theology*, seeking to show how all traditions could develop towards a closer unity, the predictable response from the orthodox of all faiths is that he has not taken their own beliefs sufficiently into account. So you can try to work towards a religion of the future, in which all faiths will be united. But what you will find is that all the faiths you are trying to unite will only be united in one thing – namely, in saying that what you are doing is quite wrong and unacceptable.

All the same, there is something odd about anyone saying, 'I have the truth, and everyone else is quite wrong', when the issues are so very obscure and when there is so much argument and dispute among equally wise and good people. It may well seem that a little agnosticism is in order. And that is where the impact of other religions has a positive role to play in British Christianity. You simply cannot agree with every religion at once, however good your intentions are. But you may well find things in other religious traditions which are good and helpful, and which help to compensate for a lack in your own tradition. You might find that, as you seek to understand another tradition, you will be able to come back to your own tradition with new eyes, and be able to put things in different ways. In other words, one faith can grow and develop and become more able to cope with the complexities of human life, as it tries to understand the insights of other faiths, to see their strength and appeal.

Lots of things have happened in this direction in recent years. In India, Catholic monks like Bede Griffiths and Abishiktananda have lived as Hindu holy men and founded ashrams, where they try to use Hindu ideas to round out their own Christian vision. Schools of Christian Zen have sprung up, and Christian yoga and meditation can be found quite frequently. It is not surprising that most of these enterprises have been undertaken by monks, who have renounced the world to pursue a sort of spiritual life which is akin to the more contemplative practices of Buddhism and Hinduism. Meditation and the pursuit of the mystical union of the soul and God have always existed in the Christian tradition. But, maybe because of Henry VIII's dissolution of the monasteries, and the Protestant emphasis on a life of active good works and industry, knowledge of that tradition has almost totally disappeared from British Christianity. So much so, that young people, looking for some sort of spiritual experience or some vision of a spiritual reality that can give deeper meaning to life, tend to go to the East or to imported gurus from the East, in their search. The sort of Christianity they have seen seems somehow shallow in its idea of union with the Divine – it too often treats God as some sort of invisible father-figure, to whom they are invited to chat, without any reasonable expectation of an answer. It has also got itself bogged down in pointless-seeming arguments about whether or not various odd miracles happened two thousand years ago, when it is apparent to all that such things can never now be established beyond doubt. It is daily seen to be undermined by writers, broadcasters and even by theologians, as the idea of a God becoming man and atoning by a bloody death for the sins of the world is said to be primitive and even immoral. So Christianity seems to be undermined by self-doubt, and to lack a basic commitment to the search for God, as a present spiritual reality which can be known or discerned. Or, perhaps more accurately, it lacks techniques for producing self-realisation and enlightenment. If you desperately want self-realisation, and all Christians give you is arguments about whether virgins can have babies, something has gone wrong somewhere.

When things look like that, then programmes like Transcendental Meditation do seem to offer the possiblility of a greater self-awareness and fulfilment, without the trappings of dogma. They fill a vacuum left in our society by a form of Christianity which has lost touch with its own deepest roots, and threatens to be simply a repressive set of doctrines of a rather archaic (ie Victorian) kind. A positive Christian response to this phenomenon is to recognise what the Christian tradition itself has to offer, in its long line of mystical teachers, and re-state this tradition in new ways. What can happen is that a positive conversation with other faiths can re-awaken lost insights or prompt new directions of thought, by reminding us that the way we look at things is inevitably partial and very much governed by the limits of our own temperament and culture.

I am not forgetting that there are issues of truth at stake, in the end. Clearly, if Christians think that there is one holy God who became man in order to die for sin, who was crucified and rose from death, then their belief is either true or false; we cannot fudge that issue. At the same time, our understanding of these things, the very way they are put, can and in fact has perceptibly changed over the centuries; it can change again, and surely will. It changes, as we perceive the different systems which people have devised for understanding themselves and their world, and for relating themselves to that transcendent ground of truth which we call God. And in this respect, our age does seem to present the possibility of a certain convergence of the great world faiths. The reason for this is that we can now perceive the global interconnectedness of human lives all over the planet. We move easily and readily from one culture to another, and our horizons are, or can be, expanded by seeing other human responses to the same basic features of human existence.

Early Christianity existed as a sect of Judaism, and was concerned with trying to get Jews to accept the fulfilment of their prophetic traditions in Jesus. When this was signally unsuccessful, the faith found a remarkable expansion throughout the Roman Empire, by assimilating many ideas from Greek, Stoic and Persian thought, and moving into a vacuum created by the demise of the old Greek and Roman gods, who had become little more than ciphers or fables by then. The missionary expansion of the church continued with great success, except where it was checked by Islam and by the religious systems of the Far East, which proved to be almost wholly resistant to this semitic import. A sea-change swept over Christianity at the Reformation and Enlightenment, when it was baptised in the waters of criticism and adopted as the motivating force behind the technological and industrial expansion of the West. But now it looks, apart from pockets of indigenous religion throughout the world, as if the major world religions have settled into their various territories, where they sit regarding one another with various degrees of hostility or exasperation.

A key feature of our age is that we can look at the whole historical process and see the complicated interplay of culture and religious symbol. We can look to the future and project the development further, realising that no one religion is going to take over the whole world in the foreseeable future. There are two extreme reactions Christians can make. One is to retreat to the fortress of church or Bible; to insist on exclusive truth and infallible certainty; and to look for the conversion of the infidel. The other is to relativise all religious claims; see them all, including one's own, as partial aspects of a truth not as yet fully known; and eschew missionary expansion, except where no great faith already exists, or insofar as it may contribute to an unforeseeable development in religious thinking, by conversation and critical exchange of ideas. The first position is very hard to maintain, when one sees the depth of spiritual perception in such traditions as Buddhism. But the second position is equally difficult, when you realise that not everybody can be equally right; and you can hardly seriously believe that your own beliefs are wrong, even if you agree that they are likely to be very inadequate. Inadequacy and error, however, are not at all the same; and you simply cannot have it all ways, and say that all is suffering (Buddhism) and that the world is good (Judaism); that there is an eternal Self (Hinduism) and that there is no self at all (Buddhism); that your personality will exist for ever (Christianity) and that it will be wholly dissolved in the Absolute (Sankara). If you seriously thought that all these views were equally wrong, you could believe none of them; and then, of course, you would not belong to a religion at all.

Very early in the history of the Christian church, the same

sort of dispute existed. Some theologians claimed that outside the church there could be no salvation. In this, they relied on texts like that from the Book of Acts: 'There is no other name under heaven by which men can be saved, but that of Jesus' (Acts 4,12). But other theologians took a more tolerant view, and pointed to the text of John's gospel: Christ is 'the light that enlightens every man who comes into the world' (John 1,9). From that, they inferred that even people who have never heard of Jesus are in fact enlightened by the eternal Christ, in a way that is appropriate for them. The historical Jesus is the culmination and the actual making flesh of the eternal Christ who is present in a hidden way in everyone. In our own day, the Catholic theologian Raymond Panikkar takes a very similar view; and Karl Rahner, perhaps the best-known modern Catholic theologian, speaks of the anonymous Christ, present with all men under many names.

The trouble with speaking about anonymous Christians or about the unknown Christ of Hinduism, as Panikkar does, is that although it is meant to be tolerant, it can actually sound quite arrogant. After all, why shouldn't a Buddhist say that all Christians are really anonymous Buddhists, and that what we call Jesus is really the hidden Buddha of Christendom? So perhaps that sort of talk is not quite so helpful as it seems at first. Then we still have the difficulty that different religions seem to believe such very different things; so, whether it sounds arrogant or not, we just cannot say that they are all true.

It seems to me what we have to do is to distinguish two things quite clearly. We must separate the question of what is true or false from the question of how a person can be saved. If we don't do that, we are in danger of saying that a person can only be saved if they believe the right things. And that would be very worrying indeed; for who among us can be quite certain that all our beliefs are true; or that at least the ones necessary to salvation have been correctly formulated? I will assume, for the moment, that 'salvation' means having an eternal relationship of knowledge and love with God. Christians claim to be saved from all that hurts and harms them, that cuts them off from the presence of God and that stunts and cripples their own lives. To be saved is to be put into a right relationship with God. This, Christians say, is brought about by God himself taking the first step, becoming man in Jesus of Nazareth, forgiving our sins and offering his love freely to us.

Now, supposing all that is true, what about all the people who never knew Jesus, or who have only heard a very distorted account of him? It is contrary to all Christian belief about a God who is love, and who goes to the furthest lengths to save sinners, to think that they will all be left without any possibility of this eternal relationship with God. And one main clue is given by the patriarchs and prophets of the Old Testament. They did not know Jesus; but surely they were given relationship with God. That leads us to say that God showed himself to them in ways which their culture allowed. If they responded to him in faith, if they lived by the best that they knew, in sincerity and love, then the saving work of Jesus was applied to them, even though they did not know it at the time. It seems plausible to generalise from the case of ancient Israel to other religious traditions, too. Then, Christians will be able to say that, if people respond in sincerity and love to the best that they know, the saving work of Christ will be applied to them. They will, perhaps only after death, be brought into personal relationship with God. They might, through no fault of their own, believe what is false; that is what is technically called 'invincible ignorance' – a false belief that cannot be overcome in practice by any argument or experience. That is how people can believe what is false – they may even believe there is no God, because the idea of God they have is indeed an immoral and unintelligible one – and still be saved by Christ.

That does not at all mean that it does not matter what you believe; as if, since you will be saved anyway, you can believe anything you like. The doctrine is that you can be saved only if you respond fully and openly to the truth as you perceive it. It does matter that you seek the truth. We might say: you will be judged by how seriously you have sought the truth; but you will not be judged on whether you have actually found it or not. It is therefore quite possible to insist on the exclusive truth of Christianity, and also to hold that all people can be saved by their response to the light that is in them, though it may include grievous errors. So the old problem of why God should have confined his revelation of truth to just one people and one period of history, and apparently left the rest to wallow in error, does not really arise. It is the nature of human life that knowledge of the truth is not simply given to everyone at birth, pure and undefiled. We have to seek it with effort and difficulty; it is discovered by some particular people at particular times, and we have to learn it from them as best we can. So it may be with God's revelation of himself. It is given at particular times and places; and we have to find our way to it with earnest striving and many frustrations. Indeed, the seeking is part of what it is to grow into salvation; for it requires of us patience and courage, sincerity and truthfulness – the virtues which predispose us to accept the grace of God. All people can be saved by God's grace and their own search for truth. But that truth, given by God at a particular time, has yet to be discovered in its fullness by patient and diligent reflection and prayer.

It is a central heresy of our culture to say that all truth is relative; that one thing may be true for me and quite another may be true for you. This absurdity destroys the very notion of truth, of there being something other than us to which we must conform, if we are to see things rightly. With typical perversity, the only claim that properly preserves human humility – namely, that our own interests, partialities and prejudices must be subordinated to what is the case – is said to be arrogance, the arrogance of claiming that we are right and others are wrong. This, however, is just the result of muddled thinking. No one can seriously believe that a belief which contradicts his or her own is just as true. The expression 'It is true for me' is self-confuting. Either a thing is true or it is not; if I believe something else, then I am just wrong. Can we imagine saying, 'Well, the earth is round to me; but it may be flat to you'? The earth is either round or flat; it cannot be both; and what you or I think about it is irrelevant. You may claim that religion and ethics is not a matter of truth at all. Very well, do not use the word 'true'; but if you use it, do not render it unintelligible by adding that empty phrase, 'for me'.

What is arrogant about thinking that what I believe is true? Indeed, 'believe' just means 'think true'. Of course, I may not wish to claim absolute or total knowledge. I may want to stress the inadequacy of my information or my uncertainty about many things. That is all right, and amounts to saying, 'I *think* it is true.' But, when all is said and done, I do think it is *true*. So it is not arrogance, it is just plain sense, for Christians to say that what they believe, they believe to be true. And anything which contradicts it must thus be false.

What often gets confused with this claim to truth, and what causes the trouble, is the claim to absolute truth. This is a very slippery phrase; but one of its meanings is that what I believe, the exact propositions I formulate, are wholly adequate representations of reality, just as they stand; and they need no further addition or transformation, to bring out the truth more clearly. This sense of 'absolute truth' needs to be distinguished from the idea of an 'irreformable truth'; that is to say, a proposition which is not in error, and which will never become false. A simple example would be the belief that 'Jesus is the son of God'. We can say that truth is irreformable, in that it will never become false, and it contains no error. But we might say that it does not give us 'absolute truth' – meaning that, though correct, it gives a very inadequate and even possibly misleading representation of the incarnation. It may suggest, for example, that Jesus is different from God as a son is different from his father. So it needs complementing by many other propositions, to bring out its meaning more fully. In this sense, to have the absolute truth would be to understand something fully and exhaustively.

Now, the point which is often overlooked is this: not only do Christians not claim to have the absolute truth, in this sense; they are bound to believe that they do not and will not ever possess it. For at the heart of Christian belief are the Mysteries of the incarnation and the Trinity; and, in saying they are Mysteries, Christians mean that the human mind is, as such, unable fully to comprehend them, though it can receive them on faith. We will never understand these things fully and exhaustively. Faced with the supreme mystery of God, we must confess that we will never in this life possess absolute truth – though we may believe many things which are irreformably true.

It is at this point that we may see it as part of the providence of God that our understanding should be increased in this age by the encounter of the great religious traditions with one another. Christians will not give up their claims to possess some irreformable truths; but they should not claim that they have a full and exhaustive understanding of the nature and purposes of God. Further, if we believe that God does exercise a providential rule over history, we will believe, I think, that he has not left himself without a witness in any age or culture. We have already noted how Christianity does not remain as a pure and completely unchanging set of beliefs. Rather, it adjusts to various cultures and takes on their forms, as it responds to new knowledge and insights and develops its understanding of its own inner possibilities further. We may well think that in the other great religious cultures, God has been forming insights into his nature and purposes which have been under-stressed or obscured in the Christian traditions. Perhaps this is the age in which those cultures can begin to exert a reciprocal influence upon one another, to give a new and fuller under-standing of God. Christians after all are called to look towards the future as the place where the glory of God will be revealed in its fullness. We each have images of Christ based upon our own understanding of history and of the churches' tradition; but we shall see Christ as he is only at the end of history; and he may be markedly different than any of us now imagine.

Maybe other religious traditions can help to show things about Christ which are obscure to us. I hardly need remind you that I am speaking as a Christian – I have never claimed anything else. So those who belong to another religious tradi-tion, or to none, will have to put things rather differently. What I am trying to convey is how the Christian faith, without imperialism and without giving up its adherence to its own irreformable truths, may now grow in understanding by encounter with the other great religious traditions of the world. And, whether you think this is a good thing or not, I believe it is something which is destined to happen in the present religiously plural culture of Britain. It will mark the next great phase in the development of religious thought in this country. It is the growing point of religious under-standing; and one of the signs of hope in a divided and violent world.

One of the encounters which is already proving most fruit-ful is the encounter between what we might call the semitic and the Indian religious traditions. The semitic religions are those which derive from the eastern end of the Mediterranean, beginning with Judaism and branching into Christianity and Islam. The Indian religions spring from the early religion of the Veda and the Upanishads, which we tend to call Hindu-ism, though it actually consists of thousands of sects. This tradition, too, has branched into offshoots which are now different religions – Buddhism, Jainism and Sikhism. There are other traditions in the world, too; notably the Chinese, Japanese and tribal religions; but the Indian and semitic are two major branches which have quite different emphases and yet remarkable overlaps and convergences.

We are most familiar with the semitic faiths, and it is characteristic of them that they look outwards to find God, to the world, to the social community and to history. They perceive God primarily as a moral will, ordaining the world to a moral purpose; a commanding and compassionate Father, who is concerned for his children, but also judges them with righteousness. If we take Judaism to represent this tradition, it is a markedly this-worldly faith. For most of the Old Testament, there was no belief in life after death at all; and it was not regarded as a very desirable state, even when they did think about it. So it found God's purpose in this world, in material prosperity and happiness, not in 'pie in the sky when you die'. It is a markedly moral faith, focusing its concern on social justice and on a community set apart to do the will of God. God is conceived as the law-giver and judge, requiring justice and mercy of his people. Perhaps the most central notion in this whole complex of thought is the idea of vocation – the idea that individuals have a special calling from God which they must pursue, on pain of disobedience and disloyalty. God is regarded as outside the self, as its judge, and as one who has a purpose in history, which will be the establishing of his Kingdom.

Most Christians are fairly familiar with all of that, although Christianity has complicated it by bringing in the idea of life after death as a major element, and by adjusting the idea of an ethnic community with its own law and its own King, so as to apply to a rather more universal ideal of a spiritual community and Kingship. However, if we look at the Indian tradition, we find something which at first seems to be the complete opposite of this scheme in almost every respect. First of all (if we take Vedantic Hinduism as our example), it is not this-worldly at all. Its goal seems to be escape from the World; and whereas the prophets of Israel got themselves mixed up in politics and the social life of the community, the holy men of India (*rishis*) retire into the forest to meditate and leave their families and societies completely. The doctrine of life after death, in the form of re-incarnation, is central to Hinduism. For everything you do in this life has its reward or punishment in a subsequent life, either in a temporary heaven or hell, or in a subsequent life on earth. Apart from this inevitable law of karma, however, there has been no idea of one righteous God in Indian tradition since the time of Varuna, a Vedic god who lost popularity quite early on in history. Indeed, there is not really one God at all; there are millions – even though sophisticated Hindus regard them all as aspects of one impersonal supreme reality, which is called Brahman.

It was this radical polytheism which the early Christian missionaries could not understand at all; and they tended to regard it as either primitive or as demonic. For a Hindu, however, there is no reason to have only one god if you can have many, each of whom represents some facet of reality which you may adore or value. It is possible to have an intensely personal relationship to one of these gods, such as Krishna or Shiva. But they are not the ultimate reality; and Brahman is an impersonal reality which includes the whole world in itself and is beyond all thoughts and images. Indian thought is thus monistic – it regards God and the world, not as two distinct things, but as one reality whose fundamental nature is spiritual. Yet there is no sense of purpose in history, no coming Kingdom or moral goal to be realised by the human community. For Vedanta, history is part of one unending cyclic process. The universe comes into being as the 'sport' or play of Brahman. In it are played out the desires of creatures, for good or ill. When they have all been played out, the universe comes to an end. But then it all begins again, exactly the same, throughout endless time. The only escape is by individual release to unity with Brahman, when your own individual self is merged with Brahman, and you become part of the one truly real, beyond desire and even knowledge.

The Indian tradition, then, does not look to find God in the events of history or as the moral orderer of society. It looks inwards to the self, the individual; and it perceives God primarily as the blissful Self or consciousness; the watcher who is unpierced by sorrow or evil, who is beyond change or action, who is without desire, eternal, changeless and pure. When we look at these two traditions, especially as I have set them out, it may seem that they are opposed at every point. The semitic tradition finds the highest purpose of human life in the subordination of the human will to a higher Divine will, in the idea of a unique vocation to be carried out on earth and fulfilled in the Kingdom of God, a community of persons. The Indian tradition finds the highest purpose of human life in absorption of the individual self in the Divine Self, in the idea of personal Enlightenment, which gives release from the cycle of rebirth and carries one beyond both community and individuality into union with the all-pervading Self. Are these not just quite different views of human nature and destiny, and of the nature of the ultimate reality?

That there are differences cannot be denied; and that is one reason why it is just silly to say that all religions are really the same. And yet there are deeper similarites, which emerge as we look at the traditions in more detail. For the semitic tradition is also aware of the eternal, the blissful and perfect Mind which is imageless and omnipresent. In the great philosophers Maimonides, Aquinas and Al Ghazali, of the Jewish, Christian and Muslim faiths respectively, these doctrines of God are clearly expounded. Whereas the semitic faiths do sometimes tend towards anthropomorphism, towards making God in the image of man, they also contain the practices of contemplative prayer and the ban on thinking of God under any image. On the other side, the Indian tradition is also aware of the moral law, though it conceives it impersonally. It is aware of Brahman as the originator of the world by will, and as having a providential aspect; even as expressing himself in personal form for the sake of his devotees. The Indian faiths, especially in their Buddhist forms, tend often towards an almost total agnosticism about the ultimate reality, calling it 'the void' or refusing to speak of it at all. Yet they also speak of it as Sat-cit-ananda, 'Being, consciousness and bliss', and find in union with it a liberation from selfish desire. Thus both traditions converge around the notion of perfect awareness as the basis of finite reality; but both approach this notion by different routes – by the prophetic discernment of the action of God in history, and by the *rishis'* discernment of the stillness of God within the self, the place of eternal bliss.

So, though each tradition has pursued a different path, traces of both – the inward path to the Self of all, and the prophetic path to the God of Love – are clearly to be found within each tradition. It is as if two streams of the same river have diverged because of culture, history and temperament, for many years, but are now flowing together again. What may come out of their meeting cannot be decreed in advance. It is not a question of starting some new, artificial religion, which picks the bits it likes out of each tradition. Nor is the future, for most people, likely to be conversion to some different tradition; for of course that will be as partial in its way as Christianity has also been. The way forward would seem to be for those who stand within the western Christian tradition (itself only one Christian tradition) really to come to know and understand what other traditions are saying, and what they can show of the fullness of God. In this encounter of differing traditions, there may be a way to help to heal old animosities, and also a way of discovering truths which have lain dormant in one's own tradition for too long.

Thus Christians may learn from the Indian tradition – indeed they are already learning – the value of meditation, of the renunciation of desire, of the search for enlightenment and self-realisation. They may learn more of the infinity and boundlessness of God, and of the way in which he can be found in all things, and within the attentive heart. They may learn to be less literalist about God and less exclusivist about salvation. All this can be learned without renouncing one's own tradition. In fact, once you see it, you may realise that these things have been in our tradition all along, but for some reason they have been so overlaid with cultural emphases of a different sort that they have been overlooked. I would say that it is now true that the best way to understand your own tradition is to immerse yourself sympathetically in someone else's, and then come back to your own with renewed vision. It may well be like seeing it for the first time.

But if Britain may now be considered a religiously pluralist society, in a real sense, that does not mean that massive conversions are about to take place to other faiths. While most people are not actively connected with a religion, British culture is very strongly Christian in its basic ideals and values, and these ideals have carried over into that secularised religion known as Humanism. Respect for individual personality; hope for the future; and the possibility of social reform, together with the necessity to care for the weak, have all carried over from a Christian context, even where they have long been divorced from it. Serious interest in other religions seems confined to ethnic groups from elsewhere, and to young people who adopt it as part of a reaction against what they perceive to be traditional values. The British religion is likely to continue to be Christian, then. The real question is, what sort of Christianity will it be? I do not think it can be the exclusivist version, which asks for too overt a commitment to too narrow a set of beliefs. I do think Christian faith is in the middle of another of those great transformations which have swept over it on many occasions previously. And it is perhaps character-istic of this one that it will be part of a general and global attempt to reintegrate the great religious visions which lie at the root of the world faiths; to let them interact with one another; to agree in the acceptance of diversity, while seeking to allow increased understanding of others to modify one's own views in unforeseeable ways. After all, this is just what the ecumenical movement between Christian churches has been doing. The dialogue of world religions is just a larger ecumenical movement, insofar as we all seek to relate to one supernatural reality which is the ground of our existence.

Once more, the Christian churches stand at the beginning of a new and exciting wave of spiritual development. It has already begun to form, as a gentle swell far out to sea, not widely perceived or felt. But as it gathers force, it may come to sweep all before it. The influx of Muslims, Sikhs, Hindus and Buddhists into Britain in this century has forced to our attention the diversity of human religious responses, and made clear some of the ways in which Christianity has been unduly restrictive or limiting in its perception of the Divine. In a recent book, Bede Griffiths, the Benedictine monk who was Prior of Farnborough Abbey, in England, and now lives in Shantiva-nam, in Tamil Nadu, India, speaking of Christianity and Hinduism, writes, 'How can we reconcile . . . the cosmic revelation of the infinite, timeless being manifesting in this world of time and change, but ultimately unaffected by it, with the Christian revelation of God's action in history, of the one, eternal Being acting in time and history and bringing this world of time and change into union with himself? This, it seems to me, is the problem of the modern world; on this depends the union of East and West and the future of humanity.' If we are disposed to think that there is something important in the human quest for self-realisation and for unity with the Divine, we might well agree that we must explore and relate all the diverse aspects of this quest as well as we can. Some of the most exciting theology is now being done in the area of inter-religious understanding. And perhaps it is worth saying that it is not enough to try to look at a whole list of different religions from the standpoint of some allegedly objective and unin-volved observer. In religion, one has to be involved before one can properly understand; so it is better to be rooted in one tradition; and from there, to seek to appreciate what another tradition can offer, as one approaches it as sensitively and patiently as one can. There will never be a 'universal mish-mash of all religions' in Britain, just as there will probably never be just one Christian church. But the next stage of our religious evolution has begun; it is one in which each tradition can grow by encounter with and, so far as may be, love of, others; in which we do not seek to condemn or convert those committed to another religious path, but grow alongside them, and value our diversity. That is a hard truth to appropriate; but it is the way forward for the Christian churches in Britain; and, at this stage in our history, it is fascinatingly within our grasp, if we only reach out for it.

Chapter Eight
A POLITICAL KINGDOM?

'Christianity is a call to personal redemption . . . a departure from the world's values . . . how far this all seems from the contemporary understanding of Christianity, with its ready endorsement of today's expectations of higher living standards, its consecration of the political moralising of the secular intelligence, its belief in a real and actual Kingdom.' So argued Edward Norman, in the provocative series of Reith Lectures he gave on the BBC in 1978, in the course of which he castigated what he called the 'politicisation of Christianity' in our age. In Chapter Four, I noted Dr Norman's refusal to identify Christianity with 'ordinary moral seriousness'. He is even more staunchly opposed to identifying Christian faith with any form of political programme. When this happens, he says, 'faith . . . becomes defined in terms of political values . . . concerned with social morality . . . reinterpreted as a scheme of social and political action.' Religious values, he holds, are properly concerned with the condition of the inward soul, the relation of that soul to eternity, and an attachment to the unseen spiritual world. Political values, on the other hand, are intrinsically changing and relative; but these days, they often aim at an increase in living standards and greater material prosperity for all, at peace and justice and love among all peoples in one big happy community. Such values, Norman argues, are illusory and can never be fully realised. They can only lead to disillusionment, since human nature is inevitably corrupt, and every political system will go terribly wrong, sooner or later. If these things are true, what more can we hope for than to turn away from this world and its political hopes altogether, to admit 'the worthlessness of all human values', and listen to the church, which 'speaks of the evidences of the unseen world, discovered amidst the rubble of this present one.'

Edward Norman's tone is apocalyptic. The world is doomed to destruction, and all religion can do is draw the soul inwardly and in quietness to the eternal and unchanging realm above all temporal hopes and fears. Believing these things, when he

153

looks around at the Christian churches in the world, and in Britain in particular, he is filled with gloom. What he sees in Britain is a collection of pinkish trendy clerics, mouthing the platitudes of peace and love, championing the claims of the poor and dispossessed, issuing reams of paper about all sorts of social and political issues, marching with CND and against apartheid; and only occasionally stopping to pray, as if by afterthought, and mainly to get new strength to go on to the next campaign or protest.

At this point, I must declare my hand. For the past few years I have been a member of the Church of England Board for Social Responsibility – worse, a member of its executive committee, and so one of those ultimately responsible for the issue of those reams of moralising paper that have so annoyed Dr Norman. We have issued statements on the Immigration Bill, on housing policy, on unemployment, on the closed shop, on nuclear deterrence and on proposals to legislate on matters of human fertilisation – among many other things. These are, of course, political issues – that is, they are matters of social organisation and policy, of the construction and maintenance of our common life in this nation. And it is certainly true that many of these documents have been quite openly critical of government policy, even though the greatest care has been taken to get a representative cross-section of political opinion on the working parties which produce the reports, and to present all available arguments as fairly as possible. So you may well ask, are these things any of the church's business? Are we not politicising the faith, and turning the house of prayer into an activist political group?

This issue has come to the fore again, in a book written by David Sheppard, Bishop of Liverpool, which he called *Bias to the Poor*; and in speeches made by the Bishop of Durham, on the subject of the miners' strike and on unemployment. What right has the church to interfere in political issues? Shouldn't it stick to its proper business of saving souls? Well, at least all this makes a change from the days, not all that long ago, when the church was accused of being the Tory party at prayer, the main prop of the Establishment and the *status quo*, and self-satisfied proclaimer of the social hierarchy in such hymns as 'The rich man in his castle, the poor man at this gate, God made them high and lowly and ordered their estate'. This image was never fully deserved, since there has long been a tradition of Christian

Socialism in Britain. But most people probably have that image; and so it looks to them as if a change has come over the churches in this century, a much greater awareness of social issues and of the possibility of social change. But again, as on so many matters, it is a change which has left many within the churches bewildered. They long for the peace of hallowed rituals and the sanctification of their lives, and are harangued by bishops about the condition of the unemployed. Outside the churches, I think most people can see the new and active social concern that many churches have; but maybe they, too, wonder just why the churches are getting involved, and whether it isn't just a compensation for lack of real faith, and a bid to get new members by any means.

There are many issues here; but let's start with the basic question of whether the churches have any right to be involved in politics. To look at that properly, we have to go back to the Old Testament, which is, after all, part of the Christian Bible – much the biggest part, in terms of size alone. The first five books of the Bible, from Genesis to Deuteronomy, make up the Torah, what we often call, rather misleadingly, the Law. These are laws which were said to have been given by God to Moses on the mountain, and they defined the life of ancient Israel. By tradition, there are 613 laws, and they cover a vast range of topics, from keeping religious festivals to not eating pork, the treatment of spots and various rules for dealing with crime and sorting out property. The most astonishing thing, for many people when they come to realise it, is that no distinction at all is made between so-called religious laws and social or moral laws. All the laws are given by God; they are certainly social, giving rules for the running of a Jewish society; and religion is not separated off as a special and non-political part of life. So the first thing to be said is that the Old Testament makes no distinction between religion and politics. It is, to repeat the words of Edward Norman, very certainly not the case that religion is concerned with the inward soul. A 'soul' is simply a living human person; and that is very much a material, psycho-physical organism – it is, as Genesis puts it, dust with God's spirit breathed into it. God is to be obeyed in all the details of social life, not just in the hidden inwardness of the soul. The prophets, who were always meddling in politics, put it very forthrightly: 'What does the Lord require of you', asks Hosea, 'but to do justice and to walk humbly with your God?'

God's law requires justice; and the prophets go so far as to say that he will not even accept sacrifices and prayers if justice is not first done.

So the Old Testament view of religion is virtually the opposite of Edward Norman's. It is concerned with social life, and it looks for the establishing of an earthly Kingdom of David or one of his descendants, and for a future of peace and justice in the Kingdom. In this, it differs markedly from many Indian religious traditions, which do agree more with Dr Norman in seeing the material world with almost total pessimism, and have, as their goal, escape from *samsara*, from the round of birth and death, into the realm of unchanging eternity, where there is no return to the sufferings of the world. The Jewish view of things is so alien to this way of thinking that I have heard one distinguished Rabbi say that his congregation would find it profoundly embarrassing to hear him preach about God, when there is so much to be done to help those who are in poverty just around the corner. The Jewish faith is intensely practical; and to be a religious Jew is to keep the Law; that is, to pursue justice, mercy and fidelity both in individual and social life. There is no division there between religion and politics.

But that is Judaism, it may be said. Christianity is something different. Well, just how different is it? Jesus was a Jew. He did not drop out of eternity, as the son of God, without being affected by his culture and the tradition which he loved. Matthew, in his gospel, makes Jesus say that every detail of the Old Testament Law must be kept (Matthew 5,18). And even if, as some claim, this was only meant until the resurrection or the birth of the church, it shows that Jesus' whole outlook was shaped by the Jewish Law. He may well have treated the Law in a humane and compassionate way – a point made by the famous quotation, 'The Sabbath was made for man and not man for the Sabbath.' But very many Rabbis who are perfectly orthodox could and did say things like that; and it seems that Jesus' arguments were not with the Law as such, but with some of its more narrow-minded and hypocritical exponents – a very different thing. When Jesus was asked which were the two most important commandments of the Law, he picked on two which are still unequivocally accepted by his followers today: 'Love the Lord your God with all your mind and heart and soul' and 'Love your neighbour as yourself.'

These are both quotations from the Old Testament Law; and they bind together the love and worship of God with a love and reverence for human life – for it is worth remembering that the Old Testament Law also says, 'You shall love the resident foreigner in your midst', not just the people you happen to like or to be related to. Furthermore, the first letter of John, in the New Testament, makes the whole thing clear beyond doubt. 'If any man says he loves God,' writes John, 'but does not love his neighbour, he is a liar.' So for the New Testament, you cannot separate the love of God from love of your neighbour. Just as much as for the Old Testament, this is not a religion of escaping from the world into some individually attained eternity. It is a religion of obeying God by loving the neighbour, the person who is made in the image of God; and by doing something practical about it; in short, by moral action.

Now, you may get as far as admitting that Christianity is not just a call to personal redemption; that it is also a call to practical love of others; and, indeed that, as James says, 'Faith without works is dead' (James 2,17). But it may be said that this still does not get us into politics. For loving your neighbour is a matter of private charity, of individual care; and it can take place in any and every political system. It is noteworthy that the New Testament contains virtually no teaching about democracy and no criticism of the Roman State, which was after all a military dictatorship. Most of the early Christians were probably slaves or people of no political importance; and it could well be held that the Sermon on the Mount calls for a degree of pacificism and total self-giving which is in fact incompatible with political responsibility. There are Christian groups, like the Amish in America, who try to live literally by the Sermon on the Mount – and that includes turning the other cheek and not resisting evil. They certainly practise love; but they remain quite aloof from the wider political process. They have to; because people who literally never resist evil obviously cannot be policemen or soldiers or ministers of defence. Nobody who refuses to judge others can be a judge or even a justice of the peace. And nobody who gives to all who ask can ever accumulate enough capital to start a business. So there are sorts of Christian life which are committed to love, but which do not involve themselves in sustaining or defending a state, especially where that state is largely populated by unbelievers. These Christians are a strange and peculiar people, strangers in the societies within which they live; and they usually do not survive for very long.

It is absolutely clear, however, that most Christians have not taken this view. Indeed, sometimes things have gone to the opposite extreme, and the church has tried to take over the world and its political processes completely. Pope Innocent III, thirteenth-century upholder of the supremacy of the papacy, said that Jesus had 'left to Peter the government, not only of the universal church, but also of the whole secular realm'; and Pope Boniface VIII, first Pope of the fourteenth century, who called himself Caesar and Emperor, held that the Pontiff is head of a universal State, and himself delegates supreme power. For, he argued, 'temporal things are ordered towards spiritual things as their end'. The same sort of thing was seen on a smaller scale in Calvin's Geneva, where Calvin wished to establish the Lordship of Christ over all life. And it is seen anywhere when Christians aim to set up a state.

No doubt there were very mixed political motives behind the medieval papal pronouncements; and few, if any, would now defend the views they held. But there is a form of thinking behind these positions which is persuasive and positive. Even if it gave rise to great abuses, still the Christian faith has reasons to regard the political processes of the world as a matter of proper theological concern. For if God has created the world as good, then it cannot be a completely pessimistic mess. If God became incarnate in the world, he gave a dignity to human nature and life in its material as well as its spiritual aspects which means that the material condition of people is important. In his lifetime, Christ healed the sick and said that he had come to pull down the rich and raise up the poor. So he was concerned with people's material needs, not just with the inward state of their souls. The church is called the body of Christ, and so it has to continue the incarnation in the world. Taken in its proper sense, which some of the medieval Popes did not seem to have fully grasped, this means that it has to accept responsibility for transforming the world into what God wants it to be, a place where every person can realise, to some extent, the gifts God has given. Above all, Christians are called to look for the Kingdom of God as a gradual transformation of the world through the influence of the church into a place where human freedom and dignity can flourish.

All these strands of thought are there in the Bible. So it is easy to see how Christians can come to think that, if they once get into positions of political power, they should seek to build a society in which God's will can be more clearly pursued. For this sort of view, Christianity is not an individualistic faith of personal salvation, but it is a search for a community within which people can worship God together and in which love can flourish freely. The job of the church is to transform the world, not to abandon it to its gloomy fate.

This sort of position is positively outlined in a document produced by the American Catholic Bishops' pastoral letter on war and peace in the nuclear age, *The Challenge of Peace*. 'Christian hope about history', they write, 'is rooted in our belief in God as creator and sustainer of our existence and our conviction that the Kingdom of God will come in spite of sin, human weakness and failure . . . The realisation of the Kingdom is a continuing work progressively accomplished', and 'the church is called to be in a unique way the instrument of the Kingdom of God in history.' The fact is that Christianity does not just look upwards, as it were, towards eternity. It also looks forwards, to the future, and to the fulfilment of the purposes of God, to a state in which tears will be swept away and injustice eliminated, when, as the Liturgy puts it, 'the whole earth will be free' and peace will reign. The very earliest Christians looked for the immanent return of Christ in glory, to usher in this Kingdom. But the mystery of God's purpose was hidden from them in its details, and Christ left the church to be the instrument of the eventual dawning of that Kingdom. If Christians think they have to work to bring in the Kingdom of God, they will be committed to political action to do so.

The Roman Catholic Church is often seen as a bastion of privilege and hierarchy, as the defender of traditional values and of social order. And yet it is within that church that the most radical theological movement of recent times has sprung up – Liberation theology. Liberation theology, as was pointed out in Chapter Four, belongs to a specific place and time; it belongs to Latin America after 1967. But its influence has reached far beyond that continent; it has given rise to Black theology, Feminist theology and other radical social movements. It even has its influence in Britain, in the work of David Sheppard and

David Jenkins. In Britain, despite the alleged conservatism of the Church of England, there is a long tradition of association between Christianity and radical or socialist political movements. The nonconformist churches have generally tended towards the left on political issues; and South Wales is a good example of the way in which the reading of the Bible led to the education of thousands of mineworkers, and to a long association between the Chapels and the Unions. Many Trade Union leaders are Christians, and they belong to this part of the British heritage. So there has never been a great conflict between socialism and Christianity in Britain. On the contrary, the two have gone naturally together, and socialism has been seen, in the words of Paul Ricoeur, as 'the efficacious, institutional and social realisation of love'. If there was to be a Christian political party in Britain, which there is not, it would almost certainly be to the left of centre – unlike the case of most European countries, where the Christian parties are rather right-wing.

Perhaps the situation has changed in recent years; and this is due, I think, to the secularisation of political life of both conservative and socialist varieties. On the right wing, a philosophy of leaving as many things as possible to market forces has led to a harsh and inhumane policy of letting the weak simply go to the wall. On the left wing, the politics of hatred and envy has led to increasing use of violence and intimidation, and an urge to destroy which is as harsh and inhumane as anything to be found among its political opponents. In this situation, it is difficult to align the churches with either camp, and a certain amount of polarisation exists, as the unacceptable face of each appears most clearly to the other. It is hard to see how Liberation theology can apply directly to this situation, in anything like its Latin-American form, where it has sprung from the slum shanties of Brazil. But that does not mean that it is wholly irrelevant, as we have seen in Chapter Four. For what it most basically points out is that Christian faith is concerned with liberation (that is a good Biblical word for salvation); and that means, liberation from everything that holds human beings back from their full potential, which prevents them realising the gifts that God gave them and meant them to use.

Of course we need to be liberated from pride, anger and despair in our own lives; for those things certainly hold us captive and prevent us from coming to know and love God. And of course it is possible to love God even when oppressed and humiliated, in prison or in poverty. But that is not the whole story. Oppression is not desirable; and God calls us to free people from it, wherever possible. There are social conditions which give rise to pride or despair more easily than others. And it is a Christian responsibility to change those conditions, as and when possible, to help people to make virtue easier. So what Liberation theology asks us to do is to identify those conditions which make liberation harder, which constrict people's lives; and then remove them. If Black people, or women, or any group of people who, in a specific society, are deprived or disadvantaged, are virtually compelled by social conditions to do things they do not want to do, and to live at a relative disadvantage to other classes of people, then Christians are bound to work to change those conditions. That is the basic Liberation theology; and, as such, it has been built into the teaching of the Roman Catholic Church in its social Encyclicals, and is mirrored in the many reports of the Anglican Board for Social Responsibility.

But there is more to Liberation theology than that; and that is what has worried people, including Pope John Paul II. For it quite explicitly uses Marxist terminology and analysis; it may indeed be called a form of Christian Marxism; and it may be wondered if these two things are compatible. Karl Marx was no friend of religion, even though it can be plausibly argued that he founded a new one himself. He described himself as a materialist, by which he meant that all intellectual ideas were determined by basic material conditions, the relations of production and exchange. Thus there is no such thing as absolute or eternal truth. As Jose Miguez Bonino, one of the most influential Liberation theologians, puts it: 'There is no truth outside or beyond the concrete historical events . . . no knowledge except in action.' This has to go for theological truths too. Like all ideologies, they in fact serve some political structure; and theology must be 'critical reflection on historical praxis'. That means that theological theories are in fact rationalisations of social processes, and they must be judged by the social conditions they support. In the light of this view, Bonino writes: 'Is it absurd to reread the resurrection today as the death of the monopolies, the liberation from hunger or a solidary form of ownership?'

I suppose, to be honest, that my reaction is to say that it *is* absurd. Once you have moved into an area where truth is relative, it seems that things can mean whatever you want them to mean. All you have to do is claim that your interpretation, however odd, expresses the social conditions of the day, or the will of the people, and you are beyond criticism. I would go further, and say that this view is actually demonic, because it puts truth at the mercy of political expediency. Marx, who was fairly clear-sighted, did not pretend that his views were true (or not when he was at his most acute). He merely said that his views would win – by the gun or sword if necessary. Beneath the relativisation of truth lies the threat of force, as the ultimate arbiter of what shall be believed. That is why Marxist-Leninism can use the words 'justice', 'peace' and 'fraternity' to mean totalitarian oppression, military expansion and support of a State secret police. Truth no longer matters, for it is determined by the concrete historical events – which means, by the society – which means, by the State – which means, by whoever happens to be in power.

It is hardly surprising, then, that Pope John Paul II, who, being Polish, knows more about Marxism in practice than most western Christians, found something objectionable in this doctrine. But there is more. One Liberation theologian says: 'Class struggle not only does not contradict the universality of love but becomes demanded by it.' It is no use appealing, as the church has traditionally done, to the common good; for there is no common good. Different classes are set irreconcilably in conflict, and there cannot be peace until all exploiting classes have been set aside. It is important to see that what Lenin meant by 'peace' was just that – the elimination of exploiting classes, the establishment of common ownership, the de-alienation of work (which means that you work because you want to, not for money) and the participation of all as political agents.

Now, I would have reservations about all this as a statement of the nature of the perfect society and of the way to achieve it. The Marxist doctrine of inevitable class conflict seems both historically inept (for no one has ever managed to define a 'class' successfully) and a recipe for continual social unrest. The idea that everyone can take a share in government is Utopian in the extreme; and in any case undesirable for the vast majority, who would much rather be doing something else. (I do not mean that as an arrogant remark; I would myself much rather be doing something else.) So there will always be someone who actually governs, and who will get some sort of reward for doing so. Are the managers of State-run enterprises any less exploitative than the managers of joint-stock companies? It may be a close run thing; but at least it is possible to leave a private company sometimes. Where the all-protective State is in control, you have to do what you are told.

The objection to these doctrines is simply that they are unworkably Utopian and socially divisive. There can be no better recipe for social disaster than a doctrine which tells you that the present system is exploitative, that it must be overthrown, by violence if necessary, and a dictatorship established which must continue until Utopia arrives. Once such a system gets started, Utopia has a strange way of getting deferred. Now it may well be said that the situation in many Latin-American states is desperate for the poor, who live in shanty-towns and who have been expropriated and driven from the land by millionaire, and often expatriate landlords. The Latin-American poor can see no way to free themselves from the social and economic exploitation of the wealthy countries except by violent revolution. And the Catholic priests who minister to them in the appalling slums do see the doctrines of Marx as having a clear relevance to that situation. They feel that something practical needs to be done, if there is to be any hope of a society in which basic needs are to be met and some measure of self-realisation made possible for all. Then, when they read in their Bibles of how God wills to liberate his people, to let them live in security and contentment, God seems to speak to them of a demand to gain freedom from oppression, as Moses led his people from slavery by the will of God.

There can be no doubt that this is a form of 'theology'; it is not just Marxist politics in disguise. These theologians have rediscovered the truth that it is God's will that those who are made in his image and for whom he gave himself on the cross should be able to achieve some sort of freedom and fulfilment in their earthly lives. It could well be said that Marx, born a Jew and baptised in infancy as a Christian, himself received much of his inspiration from the Christian tradition, partly by the way of Hegel, but partly directly from the gospels, which he apparently admired. In the work of Marx there can be found many echoes of Biblical teaching – the existence of a purpose in history which is destined for inevitable realisation; the goal of human life as the foundation of a truly just society; the brotherhood of all men (and indeed the fellowship of all men and women); and even the vocation of the 'chosen people' (the Party faithful) to lead the way. Marxism is the legacy that a complacent and insensitive Christian church has left to the world. For, insofar as the church failed to see the necessity for human liberation; insofar as it failed to see, as Bonino puts it, that 'the growth of the Kingdom is a process that occurs historically in liberation', it did become a reactionary and obstructive force to human progress. Atheistic Marxism is the judgement of history on the blindness of the children of God.

At the same time, from a Christian – and, I would say, from a truly human – point of new, Marx's rejection of God leaves his philosophy fatally flawed. Liberation theologians, or those at least who adopt his views too readily, may find themselves betraying their own cause. They insist that 'the divine can only be found through the human'; that we must make a move from the inner-personal view of faith to a public-historical view; from a metaphysical scheme to an anthropological one. We must speak of the liberation of man, and see that humanity is realised in work, in co-operative and creative action. But there is a danger here that the transcendence of God may dissolve into the future of man. It is indeed important not just to leave people in avoidable oppression or slavery. But in the end liberation is an affair of the heart, of being united to God. No process of social change is going to bring that about; and a society of material abundance and human equality can still be a profoundly empty and pointless one. One of the things essential – total reliance on God alone – is missing. In the end, Marxism turns out to be just one more Enlightenment philosophy, incorporating all the optimism of inevitable scientific and material progress, the same confidence in science – this time 'scientific materialism' – to solve our human problems. It speaks powerfully to those who are exploited and oppressed, of possible freedom and self-mastery. But it does not touch the deepest problems of all, of human meaning and destiny.

Marxism is a very uneasy bedfellow with Christian faith. We should beware when 'liberal capitalism' is condemned as exploitative and over-individualistic, whereas State socialism (the only alternative on offer) is not identified as tyrannical and anti-individualistic, subordinating the individual to the social whole and the central plan. There is a lot of work to be done yet on possible dialogue between Marxism and Christianity. But

Pope John Paul II had some justification in firing a warning-shot across the bows of Father Boff, the liberation theologian who in 1985 was asked not to publish for one year. The Canadian theologian Charles Davis has written of 'political theology' as 'theology in its entirety done politically'. That seems to me a contradiction in terms; it is rather like trying to do theology in its entirety biologically. One would hardly know where to begin. The Christian faith is concerned first with God, his will and purpose for his world. And a very strong case could be made for saying that the passionate concern for justice with which Marxism begins can only be saved from the well-meaning tyranny with which it ends by a forceful reminder that all human institutions and programmes are under the authority not of man but of God. Liberation matters; but so does truth and tolerance, and the devotion to a reality which is greater than us, yet worthy of our loyalty and unstinted allegiance. No man can be the object of such loyalty, and no abstract dialectic of history, and certainly no State. One thing Christianity bears at its heart, even when it forgets it, is that supreme authority belongs to no man, but only to God; and he is the judge of every society and system.

What Liberation theology has done is to remind Christians of the real dynamic for social justice to which they are committed. In its close alignment with Marxism, and in its Latin-American context, it cannot be simply transferred to Britain – nor would Bonino and others like him think that it could be. Yet, despite its excesses, it has something to say to the British churches; it does manifest a new thing that the Spirit is saying to the churches today.

Part of the Christian faith is the hope for God's Kingdom. And that means actively working for it by seeking to bring it nearer. The abolition of slavery was one great advance in history; and the church bears its witness today in its call for peace and for justice between the nations of the world. Yet, there is a great danger in all this, too. As Lord Acton said, 'Power tends to corrupt; absolute power corrupts absolutely.' If the church, or any part of it, identifies itself too much with God's Kingdom; if it gets too powerful as an institution; and it comes to see itself as having some sort of monopoly of truth, then it becomes repressive, censorious and corrupt. The spectacular corruption of the Borgia Popes, the horrors of the Inquisition and the sheer petty-mindedness of church bureaucracies are evident enough in Christian history for all to see. The higher the claims an institution makes for itself, the lower it seems to sink on the moral scale. And this is a lesson the churches have had to learn the hard way. It is a long time now since the Roman Church claimed political power; and few voices are now heard which would wish to subordinate the state to a hierarchical and dogmatic authority, beyond questioning or criticism. The days of an authoritarian political church have gone for ever, and with it any false hopes that some human institution could bring about the Kingdom of God in history.

So, from the very first, Christianity has oscillated between thinking that the Kingdom could never come by human action at all, that the world is too corrupt to bother much about; and thinking that the Kingdom will come if only we try a little harder. But the truth lies in the tension between these two extremes. The Christian faith does hold out a hope for the world, a hope that human lives will be brought to fulfilment. It is a complete mistake to think of this fulfilment as only after death or in some purely spiritual realm. We are talking about the realisation of personal gifts and talents, the fulfilling of material needs, for people, especially the poor, now. When members of the Church of England sing at Evensong, 'He shall cast down the mighty from their seats, and the rich he shall send empty away', the words do not perhaps penetrate very far. Still, they are undeniably there, and they must make the rich and mighty just a little uncomfortable. This is God's world, and he wants us to achieve fulfilment in it, to cherish and care for it; to live in peace and care for one another. In a complicated world like ours, such things need to be achieved by social planning and organisation. They cannot be left to the whims of individuals. So the law must be used, wherever possible, not only to preserve life and property, but to assure the poor of sustenance and the sick of care and treatment.

If the churches in Britain appear to be moving to the left, it is because of their fear that Christian values of care for the poor and respect for every human life, as made in God's image, are under threat. It is equally true that such values would be under threat from the forces of the extreme left, which would seek to establish a tyranny of control and a suppression of individual initiative and freedom. So the churches find a political role in trying to stand for life, for peace and for equal justice, wherever such things are under threat. They stand for the goal that God puts before us to strive for, the goal of a community bound together in love.

At the same time, there is no basis in Christianity for easy optimism about the future. Christians are obliged to strive for the Kingdom – otherwise, it is a waste of time praying that it may come. But they are also deeply aware of sin – that is of the forces of evil, hatred and violence which threaten every human community. So they do look for the fulfilment of God's Kingdom in a world beyond this one, where sin and greed can be finally overcome by love. That does not mean they do not care what happens now. But it does mean that they will not despair if their plans go wrong; for they believe that good will not be finally defeated, that there will be a consummation of temporal events in the realm of eternity. In this way, Christian hope cannot be finally defeated, and it impels believers always to strive for good, without being anxious about how much of it is going to be achieved, by their own efforts.

If this is true, we might expect the churches to exercise a primarily critical role in society, pointing out where peace and justice are under threat. But we might not want them to take power themselves, since we can trust them no more than we can trust anyone else. The churches are at their best when they are witnesses to hope and to justice, not judges of the hearts of men and women or rulers of temporal Kingdoms.

Is faith then being politicised? Is it being reduced to a programme of political action? I can see little evidence that this is the case. What is happening is that there has been a rediscovery of the moral demands made by the teachings of Jesus and of the Bible, and a realisation that these involve social as well as personal action. When Karl Marx said that religion was the opium of the people, he meant that it offers an illusory consolation to those who have no hope in the world. There is that danger in religion; but it is very far from the Christian basis of faith, which teaches that God actually entered into the world to transform it, in the person of Jesus. Jesus himself did not start a political party – such things did not exist. But he did start a new sort of community, the church, which from the very first aimed at brotherhood, equality, at the sharing of all things in common and at care for the poor and bereaved. Maybe the churches in Britain today are back in something like the position of that early church. They are no longer the wealthy representatives of the *status quo*. Rather, they exist almost as alternative societies with a distinctive life-style. The old monastic vows of poverty, chastity and obedience do not attract everybody today. But they might be reinterpreted in a way which is deeply relevant to today's world. A commitment to poverty would be a commitment to a simple life-style, perhaps to living in new styles of community, where goods are shared in common, so that any surplus can be used to feed the poor of the earth. Poverty is not accepted for its own sake; but out of a deep belief that anything which exceeds that which is necessary for life is theft from God, who gives us money to be used in his service, and not for wasting on luxuries. Maybe the churches, or groups of people within the churches, are rediscovering today these ancient truths, of a simple life in common, in the service of others.

Then we might speak, not of chastity, in the sense of not getting married, but of fidelity in our personal relationships. The marriage commitment of respect and care and companionship until death, whatever happens, whether better or worse, is one that can be extended to many human relationships; an absolute commitment of fidelity which will not be broken, and which alone gives a security to human relationships upon which wider values can then be built. And finally we might speak, not so much of obedience, which gives the impression of blind acceptance of authority, as of responsibility for the wider community and for the earth itself. Our own self-interest must be subordinated to the good of others; and our concern must be for all that makes for wholeness, both in human being and in all created things. Sometimes people think that those who are concerned for animals, for ecology or for healthy eating are cranks and fools. But Christians should perhaps be counted in their number – fools for the sake of Christ, whose will it is to bring all creation to its proper fulfilment.

This idea, of small groups of people committing themselves to lives of poverty, fidelity, responsibility and sharing, is a hard one to put into practice; it is perhaps a counsel of perfection; and it needs a stronger, sterner institutional backing to keep it alive. What we can say of the churches is that, flawed and imperfect as they are, they do keep alive these ideals, of living within the wider society as witnesses to love. And, it is most important to see, they accept that they will fail and need forgiveness. They will try and fail and try again; and only insofar as they rely totally on God will they in any way succeed.

As we look around at the churches in Britain, we see a strange mixture of an ancient, expensive and decaying heritage of cathedrals, choir schools and canonries with a proliferation of more informal groups of people seeking an alternative life-style in simplicity and poverty. It is no accident that Edward Norman speaks from the ancient privilege of a Cambridge college, the oldest and most conservative of them all; or that Bishop Sheppard speaks out of years of ministry in the East End of London and in Liverpool, most troubled of all British cities. The church exists in both these worlds; it speaks from an often idealised past and to an uncertain future. The strains and difficulties it contains are simply those of being human; in religion, as elsewhere, there is no growth without conflict. But there is something new in existence; a new appreciation of the importance of this world, for which God gave himself on the cross; a widening of moral awareness; a new commitment to social justice as part of the Gospel. The church indeed speaks of eternity; but it also seeks to enshrine eternity in time, to shape the temporal to express the eternal, and to build human society so that it, too, expresses the love and justice and compassion of God. In these stirrings of a deep and invincible feeling that we are called to create a new society of justice and peace, there is in fact a revival of true religion, of the sense of the sacredness of the world at its core. And I hazard the thought that it is only the churches which can deliver us from a facile Utopianism on the one hand and from a despairing slide into destructive violence on the other. A religion founded on the cross will know that there is no easy way to a just society and that those who take the sword will perish by the sword. A religion founded on the resurrection will know that it is the vision of hope and the unfaltering commitment to love which will bring the Kingdom near in the fallen world. It is more than anything else through a renewed moral commitment that the churches in Britain may find their true place in our society, through being, quite simply, communities of love. That possibility is real and urgent. Can it be realised?

I suppose the answer to that is, only if people are prepared to start to make the experiment. And that is where the question of religion becomes no longer abstract and theoretical, but a challenge to personal commitment, to a life of discipleship which flows from the vision of hope.

Maybe that is where Christian faith should start, and where it always really has started, in practice. Not with some austere intellectual theory, and not with speculations about the existence of a supernatural being. But with a commitment to a form of life in which self-interest, envy, hatred and pride may be set aside; to the building-up of a community of mutual service and responsibility. Many Christians would say that it is only in such a community that faith can come alive. It is as such a life is lived that the presence of a challenging and sustaining God becomes real. Because trying to live out that life actually puts you in touch with the deepest resources and also with the deepest conflicts in your own personality. It is then, a Christian might say, that God speaks and that we can respond. It is then that theology becomes real. And although I love the great cathedrals, the music of beautiful choirs and the majestic language of the Prayer Book, I believe the heart and the future of Christianity is to be found in such small communities, trying to make the Kingdom of justice and peace real in their own lives and to make a little of God's future real in every present time.

BIBLIOGRAPHY

This is a list of selected books by the authors mentioned in the text which may suggest useful further reading.

Chapter One

John Gladwin: *God's People in God's World* (Inter-Varsity Press, 1979). *Conscience* (Grove Books, 1977). (Ed) *Dropping the Bomb* (Hodder and Stoughton, 1985).

David Martin: *Sociology of English Religion* (Heinemann, 1967). *Breaking of the Image* (Blackwell, 1982). *Unholy Warfare* (Blackwell, 1983).

Peter Clarke: *West Africa and Islam* (Edward Arnold, 1982). *West Africa and Christianity* (Edward Arnold, 1986). *Black Paradise; the Rastafarian Movement* (Aquarian Press, 1986).

Lesslie Newbigin: *Christian Witness in a Plural Society* (BCC, 1977). *The Other Side of 1984* (WCC, 1983). *Unfinished Agenda* (SPCK, 1985).

Sources for Statistics: *UK Christian Handbook 1983* (Evangelical Alliance, 1983). *University of Leeds Sociology Dept Research Paper* (Leeds, 1982). *Gallup Poll*, 1968. *Church House*, 1983. *Catholic Media*, 1984. *Les Valeurs du Temp Present* (Presses Universités de France, 1983).

Chapter Two

Jacques Monod: *Chance and Necessity* (Collins, 1972).

Fritjof Capra: *The Tao of Physics* (Fontana, 1976).

John Polkinghorne: *The Way the World Is* (SPCK, 1983). *The Particle Play* (W. H. Freeman, 1979). *The Quantum World* (Longman, 1984). *One World* (SPCK, 1986).

David Bartholomew: *God of Chance* (SCM Press, 1985). *Stochastic Models for Social Processes* (John Wiley, 1978).

Arthur Peacocke: *Creation and the World of Science* (Clarendon Press, 1979). *Science and the Christian Experiment* (OUP, 1973). *Introduction to the Physical Chemistry of Biological Organisation*, (OUP, 1986).

Paul Davies: *God and the New Physics* (Dent, 1983). *Forces of Nature* (CUP, 1979).

Richard Dawkins: *The Selfish Gene* (OUP, 1976). *The Blind Watchmaker* (Longman, 1986).

Alister Hardy: *The Spiritual Nature of Man* (Clarendon Press, 1979). *The Living Stream* (Collins, 1965). *The Divine Flame* (Religious Experience Research Unit, 1978).

W. H. Thorpe: *Biology and the Nature of Man* (OUP, 1962).

P. W. Atkins: *The Creation* (W. H. Freeman, 1981).

Hugh Montefiore: *The Probability of God* (SCM Press, 1985).

Rupert Sheldrake: *A New Science of Life* (Blond and Briggs, 1981).

Chapter Three

A. J. Ayer: *Language, Truth and Logic* (Pelican, 1971). *Part of My Life* (OUP, 1978). *The Central Questions of Philosophy* (Weidenfeld and Nicolson, 1973). *More of My Life* (OUP, 1985). *The Problem of Knowledge* (Pelican, 1956). *Philosophy in the Twentieth Century* (Allen & Unwin, 1982).

R. G. Swinburne: *The Coherence of Theism* (OUP, 1977). *The Existence of God* (OUP, 1979). *Faith and Reason* (OUP, 1981).

Ludwig Wittgenstein: *Philosophical Investigations* (Blackwell, 1974). *Lectures and Conversations on Aesthetics, Psychology and Religious Belief* (Blackwell, 1966).

D. Z. Phillips: *The Concept of Prayer* (Blackwell, 1981). *Faith and Philosophical Enquiry* (Routledge and Kegan Paul, 1970). *Death and Immortality* (Macmillan, 1970).

Michael Dummett: *Frege* (Duckworth, 1973). *Thomas Aquinas: Summa Theologiae, Vols 2–4* (Eyre and Spottiswoode, 1964). *Truth and other Enigmas* (Duckworth, 1978). *Elements of Intuitionism* (OUP, 1977).

Keith Ward: *Rational Theology and the Creativity of God* (Blackwell, 1984). *The Concept of God* (Blackwell, 1974). *Holding Fast to God* (SPCK, 1982). *The Living God* (SPCK, 1984).

J. L. Mackie: *The Miracle of Theism* (OUP, 1982).

P. T. Geach: *God and the Soul* (Routledge and Kegan Paul, 1969).

I. T. Ramsey: *Religious Language* (SCM Press, 1957).

A. N. Whitehead: *Process and Reality* (Collier Macmillan, 1980).

Brian Davies: *Thinking about God* (Geoffrey Chapman, 1985).

A. Plantinga and N. Wolterstorff: *Faith and Rationality* (Notre Dame, 1983).

Chapter Four

Richard Harries: (Ed) *Reinhold Niebuhr and the Issues of our Time* (Mowbray, 1986). *Christianity and War in a Nuclear Age* (Mowbray, 1986). *Should a Christian Support Guerrillas?* (Lutterworth Press, 1982). *Being a Christian* (Mowbray, 1981). *The Authority of Divine Love* (Blackwell, 1983).

Edward Norman: *Christianity and the World Order* (BBC, 1978). *Church and Society in England* (Clarendon Press, 1976). *The English Catholic Church in the Nineteenth Century* (Clarendon Press, 1984).

G. Hughes: *Authority in Morals* (Sheed & Ward, 1983).

Charles Elliott: *The Development Debate* (SCM Press, 1971). *Praying the Kingdom* (Darton, Longman and Todd, 1985). *Comfortable Compassion?* (Hodder and Stoughton, 1986).

Don Cupitt: *The World to Come* (SCM Press 1982). *The Leap of Reason* (Sheldon Press, 1976). *The Sea of Faith* (BBC, 1984). *The Crisis of Moral Authority* (SCM Press, 1985).

John Macquarrie: *Three Issues in Ethics* (SCM Press, 1970).

I. T. Ramsey: *Christian Ethics and Contemporary Philosophy* (SCM Press, 1966).

Renford Bambrough: *Moral Scepticism and Moral Knowledge* (Routledge and Kegan Paul, 1979).

Alasdair Macintyre: *After Virtue* (Duckworth, 1981).

Philippa Foot: (Ed) *Theories of Ethics* (OUP, 1967).

Keith Ward: *The Divine Image* (SPCK, 1976).

Chapter Five

Morna Hooker: *The Son of Man in Mark* (SPCK, 1959). *The Message of Mark* (Epworth Press, 1983). *Studying the New Testament* (Epworth Press, 1979). *New Wine in Old Bottles* (University of London, 1984).

David Stacey: *Interpreting the Bible* (Sheldon Press, 1976).

Rudolf Bultmann: *Jesus Christ and Mythology* (T. & T. Clark, 1980).

Geza Vermes: *Jesus the Jew* (Fontana, 1976). *Jesus and the World of Judaism* (SCM Press, 1983). *Dead Sea Scrolls in English* (Penguin, 1970).

Graham Stanton: *Jesus of Nazareth in New Testament Preaching* (CUP, 1975). (Ed) *The Interpretation of Matthew* (SPCK, 1983).

Dick France: *Jesus and the Old Testament* (Inter-Varsity Press, 1971). *Tyndale Commentary on Matthew's Gospel* (Inter-Varsity Press, 1986). *Gospel Perspectives* (JSOT Press, 1980).

Chapter Six

David Jenkins: *The Contradiction of Christianity* (SCM Press, 1985).

Ted Harrison: *The Durham Phenomenon* (Darton, Longman and Todd, 1985).

John Macquarrie: *In Search of Deity* (SCM Press, 1984). *In Search of Humanity* (SCM Press, 1981). *Principles of Christian Theology* (SCM Press, 1966). *An Existentialist Theology* (Greenwood Press, 1979).

Rowan Williams: *Eucharist Sacrifice* (Grove Books, 1982). *Resurrection* (Darton, Longman and Todd, 1982). *The World of Knowledge* (Darton, Longman and Todd, 1979).

Stephen Sykes: *Christian Theology Today* (Mowbray, 1983). *The Identity of Christianity* (SPCK, 1984). (Ed) *Karl Barth* (OUP, 1980).

Colin Gunton: *Becoming and Being* (OUP, 1978). *Yesterday and Today* (Darton, Longman and Todd, 1983). *Enlightenment and Alienation* (Marshall, Morgan and Scott, 1985).

Chapter Seven

John Hick: *Christianity at the Centre* (Macmillan, 1968). *Christ in a Universe of Faiths* (Quaker Universalist Group, 1982). *Problems of Religious Pluralism* (Macmillan, 1985). *Death and Eternal Life* (Macmillan 1985). *Evil and the God of Love* (Macmillan, 1985).

Cantwell Smith: *Towards a World Theology* (Macmillan, 1981).

Raymond Panikkar: *The Unknown Christ of Hinduism* (Darton, Longman and Todd, 1964).

Bede Griffiths: *The Marriage of East and West* (Collins, 1982).

Chapter Eight

David Sheppard: *Bias to the Poor* (Hodder and Stoughton, 1984).

Haddon Willmer: (Ed) *Christian Faith and Political Hopes* (Epworth Press, 1979). *The Challenge of Peace* (*US Bishops' Pastoral Letter*) (SPCK, 1983).

Jose Miguel Bonino: *Revolutionary Theology Comes of Age* (SPCK, 1975). *Towards a Christian Political Ethics* (SCM Press, 1983).

INDEX